John W. Carpenter's
T·E·N·N·E·S·S·E·E
COURTHOUSES

A celebration of 200 years of county courthouses

John W. Carpenter, Photographer and Publisher
Michael Emrick AIA, Text and Historical Photographs

©Copyright 1996. John W. Carpenter and Michael Emrick, AIA.
All Rights Reserved.

Library of Congress Catalog Card Number: 96-96799

ISBN: 0-9621337-1-X

Printed in the United States of America

John W. Carpenter, Publisher
P.O. Box 804
London, Kentucky 40741

DEDICATION

To

My Father and Mother,

W. S. Carpenter and Bess Carpenter

and

My Wife's Father and Mother

Lee Bisset and Pearl S. Bisset

Introduction

As you look at these photographs—the one of your courthouse as well as those of others—it will be apparent that I am not yet out of the ranks of amateur photographers. I hope that by the next publication I will have eased a little closer to a professional status. A true professional could not have enjoyed this project more than my wife and I as we toured this marvelous state. Actually finding the towns in some cases, and then locating the courthouse was a lot of fun. We would say almost simultaneously, "beautiful"—"nice"—or "good grief." We were about two years getting all 95 of the Tennessee county courthouses.

Lighting is of prime importance to any photographer. The ideal way to photograph a project like this is to go into a town, check the time of day at which the best lighting occurs, and then wait for the sky to be filled with beautiful clouds. This, could of course, take weeks at one location. Since the time required to do it this way was prohibitive, your courthouse may have been shot in very poor or flat lighting with a "chalk" sky as a result. For this I apologize. If you are a serious camera buff, you will notice that all the photographs have been perspective corrected (walls vertical), using a view camera with full movements, front and rear.

After something over 8000 miles of driving, it became apparent why we could not find a book featuring all 95 Tennessee courthouses. (There was a paper back published some years ago but it did not represent the scope of this book.) It is a huge undertaking! Why would anyone other than a candidate for a state-wide political office visit 95 county seats? This is a big, beautiful, highly diversified state. If you drive from Mountain City to Memphis to Tiptonville, back and forth several times, you will see a panorama of terrain, agriculture, architecture, industry, plant life, people and politics that is unbelievable! I doubt that you will ever again say "thank God for Arkansas." Few places will top what you have seen.

After having done this same book on Kentucky, we gave up trying to eliminate or hide antennae, wires, traffic signs, traffic lights, telephone booths, and trash cans from the camera. If the fiscal court and the "locals" did not object, why should we? Taking this into account, we tried to locate an optimum angle for the available lighting with complete disregard for any man-made clutter. It is doubtful that anyone actually notices these things since their accumulation has been so gradual. I am sure that at the turn of the century all were untrammeled; and as the state of the art of communication and electronics developed, each bureaucracy wanted their own antenna, etc...

In reviewing all the 95 courthouses, it becomes obvious that the older ones of classical design are more handsome and elegant than some of the more modern structures, post-1930,—no offense intended to the architectural community. I think that it behooves all fiscal courts, officials, and the voting public to take a long, hard look before razing old buildings for something modern, just for the sake of being modern. Several counties have met the need for expansion by retaining the classic and taking the overflow of bureaucracy to a new annex. Good examples are Knox and Roane counties. Knox preserved and still uses the old building, but put up a splendid concrete, steel and glass structure for the overflow. Roane county went a different route; they saved the original, which I think now houses a museum and shops. Then, they built a beautiful building of classic design large enough to house everything. They also made an excellent move to eliminate clutter. Many Tennessee courthouses have been placed in the National Register of Historic Places and will probably be preserved. To those of you who have tried to preserve your old courthouses, but failed, thanks for trying.

There is some interesting trivia about the county-county seat relationship. Only one county seat takes its name directly from the county, and that is Loudon. Seven others use the county names but add a "ville", "burg" or "boro". There are 14 county seats named after counties, but not their own county. Some of these are neighboring counties, and some are 3oo miles apart. It would be interesting to know how these all originated. In county seat names there are 25 "villes", 10 "tons", 5 "boro", 5 "burgs", 3 "cities", 3 "dens", and two each of "towns, "sons", and "chesters". Thirty courthouses have public clocks; 28 of them are of the "four faced" types. Of the 30, 16 were stopped or had the wrong time, and 4 had different times on the four faces. The cupolas of Fentress, Roane, and Meigs seem to have been designed for clocks but none existed.

We had an interesting photographic experience in Carroll county. Every photographer is always looking for that special lighting which usually comes for a few seconds just before dark; subjects tend to, or appear to, "glow". Some call it "sweet light", "soft light" or "quiet light". I thought I had it in spades on this courthouse. The monument in front started to glow in the ground glass. It wasn't until I developed the negative that I realized I was badly fooled, the flood light, which comes on at dark, came on. Rather than drive back to Carroll county and reshoot, I decided to let it be printed as is.

Another unusual occurrence was at Crockett county. I think the local science class was having a contest, "who could package the egg" the most successfully; of course, it had to be dropped off the courthouse roof. I didn't stay to see who won, but I'll bet the participants will remember when they see this photograph.

When we arrived in Altamont, we began hunting the courthouse. Not to be found. Finally we saw a trailer in front of a local church with a courthouse sign on it. Seems as though their courthouse had burned some time before, with nothing remaining but a low wall and lots of weeds. We took a picture of the remains and decided to use it. Before publication time we heard that Grundy county had a new courthouse. We drove back to Altamont (no easy town to get to) and met with quite a shock. Here, in a county with one of the smallest populations in the state, sat one of the most beautiful classically designed courthouses in the state of Tennessee. Congratulations and hats off to the people of Grundy and Altamont.

Those of you who have seen the Kentucky book will have noticed the Kentucky Bicentennial "Logo" on the dust jacket. We had hoped for the same for this Tennessee book. The Tennessee Bicentennial Commission had rules and requirements that prohibited this small-town country boy from using their Logo. Their requirements: understanding two pages of rules, filling out a six-page questionnaire, and last but not least, requiring a $2,000.00 application fee. All this guaranteed nothing but the privilege of applying. NO WAY.

There are seven county seats with populations less than 1000 and another fourteen that are less than 2000. This represents almost 25% of the county seats with less than 2000 people. These county seats and courthouses carry out the same bureaucratic functions as the ones with over a million population; the only difference is the volume of work being handled. In the beginning, most counties were sized so that a resident could get to the seat of government and home again in the same day on horseback. Repetition of services in some of the smaller counties could eventually lead to the need for consolidation. I use that word softly because the furor that would be caused by such a suggestion, if made seriously, is beyond comprehension. If economics force such in the future, this book will be a record of "the way it was" in the 1990's. If any written material or photographs in this publication offend anyone, please accept this as my formal apology.

—John W. Carpenter

ACKNOWLEDGEMENTS

I would like to express my sincere thanks to the following:

- Michael Emrick, AIA., co-author and architectural historian for his splendid work and research for the text of this book.
- Bennett H. Wall, University of Georgia, for suggestions and sharing his vast knowledge of book publishing.
- John E. Cornett, Civil Engineer, for his helpful suggestions and word processing.
- Kelly Kincer and Sharon Goode, for their typing of labels and help in mailing brochures.
- Gregory D. Forderhase, Knoxville Attorney, for his help and legal assistance.
- Judy Hamilton, Selmer, Tennessee, for her untiring efforts to get information on McNairy to us.
- To the many police officers who "looked the other way" when I had to park illegally to get a picture.
- And to my very patient wife who went with me on all the travelling, text proofing and tolerated my many hours of absence in the darkroom.
- Then, thanks but no thanks to the Tennessee Bicentennial Commission who made it impossible for me to use their bicentennial logo on the cover of the book.

—John W. Carpenter

Preface

In celebration of Tennessee's Bicentennial, this work is intended to chronicle as completely as possible the numerous county courthouses constructed over the state's 200-year history. Using any and all available resources, in particular historic views, the result is a comprehensive visual survey of the development and evolution of the county courthouse in Tennessee as well as a recording of the number, styles, dates, and where possible, designers of both past and present county courthouses in each of Tennessee's 95 counties. As thorough a search as was possible has been made for information on the past and current county courthouses of each county through the use of county histories, articles, essays, unpublished studies, newspaper accounts, and manuscript and photograph collections. Extremely useful were the extensive photographic and manuscript holdings of the Tennessee State Library and Archives. In particular, their special project "Looking Backward," designed to document historic photographs in various private hands in all 95 of Tennessee's counties, produced a number of real treasures.

A few comments on the organization of this book may also be in order. We begin with introductory sections on the history of Tennessee's county courthouses and Tennessee and its state capitols. Following these are individual sections for each county. Paired are a brief history on the development of each county's courthouses facing a photograph of the current county courthouse. Included are single pages for two Tennessee counties which no longer exist - Tennessee County, which was dissolved at the time of statehood and became Robertson and Montgomery Counties, and James County, the only county to have gone bankrupt. Research source notes, photo credits and an extensive bibliography (each organized by county) follow. In the bibliography a code has been assigned to each reference. Rather than cite the entire source each time, it is this code which has been used in the notes as well as in the photo credits where appropriate.

Very special thanks are in order to Bill Hollings (of the Office of Legal Services for the Tennessee General Assembly), who proof-read the text, provided useful comments and corrections, and contributed information on the structure of the state and county government. Also, to the staff of the Tennessee State Library and Archives for their assistance in locating useful photographs in their various holdings. Also of great assistance in this project are the numerous individuals - county historians, county executives, sheriffs, registrars and other individuals - who took time to answer questions and provide information for their particular counties. In particular I would like to thank J.A. Dillon Jr. (Warren County), R.C. Forrester (Obion County), Dale Gentry (Standard Banner, Jefferson County), Judy Hamilton (McNairy County), John Kivett (Claiborne County), Beulah Linn (Sevier County), Walter Lumsden Jr. (Monroe County), Bonnie Heiskell Peters (Obion County), T.O. Perkins (Humphreys County), Richard B. Pierce (Pickett County), Tommy Prather (McNairy County), Marion Presswood (Polk County), Yolanda Reid (Robertson County), E.R. Walker III (Cocke County).

I also want to thank Connie Wallace for helping get met into doing this book as well as The Omni for their assistance in laying out the final dust jacket design.

Finally, many thanks to my many friends and business clients who, during my research and preparation of this book, were gracious in putting up with me as I sometimes ignored them or pushed the limits of their project deadlines.

■   Michael Emrick

Tennessee's County Courthouses

Introduction

The county courthouse is not only the focal point of each county, it is also the symbol of the community. As such, it has often been designed to present an image of security, prosperity and stability. During the course of researching Tennessee's county courthouses, I have been pleasantly surprised at the wide range and quality of designs completed over the 200 years of Tennessee's statehood.

In attempting to present an essay on, more than an architectural history of these courthouses, I have often wished for more information than "a brick courthouse was constructed..." in my searches through county histories and records. The results are unfortunately uneven with respect to how each county has been covered-- some county's courthouses being exceptionally well documented and others less so. Of one thing I can be certain is that you, the reader, will come forward with corrections, questions, other sources of information and possibly historic photographs of courthouses long since gone. This I welcome and with it, the hope of updating this book in the future.

Tennessee's courthouses, I have found, can be characterized as modest and generally less excessive with respect to detail and decoration. This is very much in keeping with the largely rural character of many counties. There are, however, grand and imposing structures built in the late 19th and early 20th centuries, which have been constructed to house county administrative offices and courtrooms. These are the courthouses many people want to look at and talk about. But they are not the full story of Tennessee's county courthouses.

Initially, Tennessee was the westward extension of North Carolina to the Mississippi River. The area quickly became a target of land speculation for those seeking opportunity and fortune further west. The first attempt at statehood and separation from North Carolina occurred in 1784 with the creation of the short-lived State of Franklin. What was eventually to become the state of Tennessee was first territorially recognized with the creation of the North Carolina county of Washington in 1777 (the first political subdivision to be named after George Washington). All of Tennessee's counties have been created out of Washington County.

By statehood in 1796, 10 counties had already been established in this area by North Carolina. The first counties established by the new state in April of 1796 (just prior to formal statehood) were Carter, Montgomery and Robertson. The last county to be formed was Pickett County in 1879. Only 12 counties were formed after the Civil War, one of these being James County, which was dissolved in 1919. Today, the largest county in area is Wayne (734 square miles), while the smallest is Trousdale (114 square miles). Between 1778 and today, Tennessee's counties built over 350 courthouses which are the subject of this book.

The Origins of County Government

The origins of our county government system can be traced back to developments in Virginia and Massachusetts. These two colonies were the inheritors of the English county ("shire") court system, and it was passed on through them. Virginia, oriented towards the rural, plantation

Tennessee's political divisions in 1783.

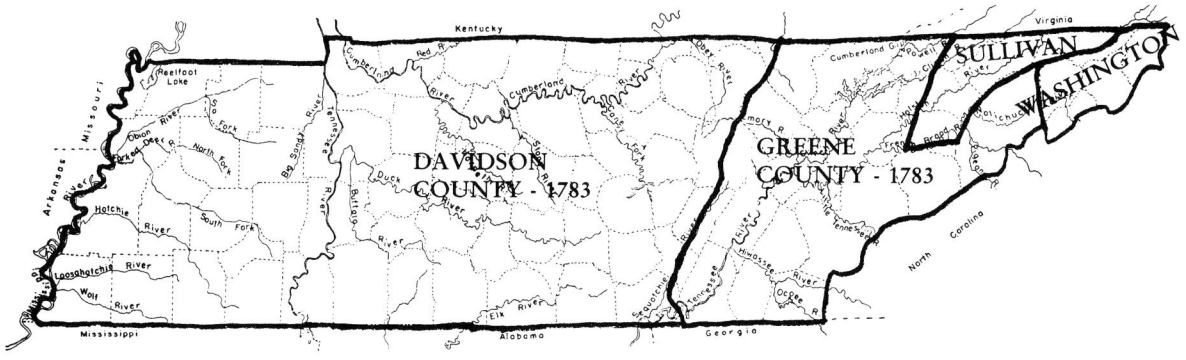

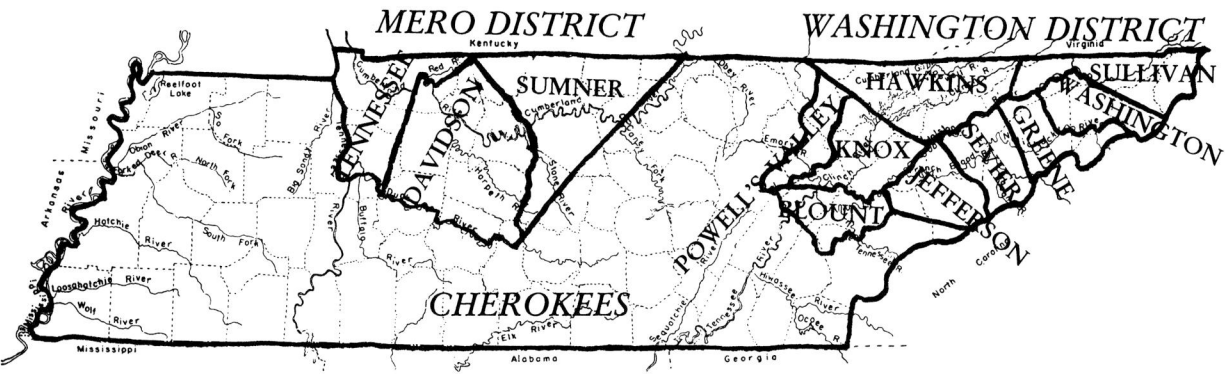

Tennessee's political divisions in 1796, just prior to statehood.

system, had no need for the form of town government developing further north in New England, where congregation in towns, became focus of the government. Virginia led in adopting a county system, passing an act in 1634 promulgating seven "shires" to be "governed as the shires in England." In 1643 the Massachusetts Bay colony followed suit.

Four patterns of county government developed: (1) the New England model, with the county subordinate to the town; (2) the New York model, where each county had a board of supervisors, all chosen by their respective townships; (3) the Pennsylvania model of elected county officials; and, finally, (4) the Virginia model, with the county as the most powerful form of local government. Generally most southern states (including Tennessee) and some western states have followed this last model.[1]

Evolution of County Government In Tennessee

The design and growth in size of Tennessee's county courthouses have been affected by the number and type of county offices and courts established in each county. These county offices and courts, in turn, have varied during the state's 200 year history. Two courts were convened with the creation of a county--the Quarterly Court and the Court of Pleas and Sessions. The Quarterly Court was basically the governing body for the county. The Court of Pleas and Sessions was the judicial court. Both of these courts, together with offices for the appropriate court and county officials were to be housed in the county's courthouse, located in the town designated as the county seat. Authority for all county offices and courts derives from the Tennessee Constitution and how they currently exist is the result of modifications to the governmental structure created by each of Tennessee's three constitutions.

The Constitution of 1796 provided for "such superior and inferior courts of law and equity, as the legislature shall, from time to time, direct and establish." This provision resulted in a state Supreme Court, a statewide system of circuit courts, and a county court in each county. In addition to these courts, Article V of the 1796 Constitution also provided for justices of the peace in each county and provided that "each court shall appoint its own clerk." Article VI went on to provide for the county offices of sheriff, coroner, trustee, register, ranger and constable.

Tennessee's Constitution was revised in 1835 to reflect the state's transition from frontier to settled society. The Constitution of 1835 extensively revised the judicial article, specifying for the first time the structure of the Supreme Court, providing for courts of law and equity, recognizing justice of the peace courts and establishing "corporation" or municipal courts for the first time. The new judicial article also recognized the development of separate clerk's offices for the circuit, chancery and county courts. The local government article was revised to provide for the popular election of the county sheriff, trustee and register, while continuing the election of the coroner and ranger by the justices of the peace.

The state's constitution was next revised in 1870 due to the profound changes in Tennessee resulting from the War Between the States, but few changes were made in the judicial or county governmental structure. The long-established system of the organization of the courts by circuit was formally recognized, and a system for electing justices of the peace and constables by district was established.

This structure of government remained largely unchanged until 1978, when a series of amendments to the 1870 Constitution abolished the traditional offices of ranger, justice of the peace, coroner and constable, replacing these with new positions of county legislative body and county executive. The existing office of county clerk also became a constitutional position. This is the judicial and county government structure we have today. Stewart County was the last county to maintain a combined judicial and legislative body, changing only in 1978.

The effect of these changes over the two centuries of courthouses has been dramatic. When Tennessee became a state with a population of some 85,000, newly formed counties could be organized in one of the larger houses in the new county. Dixonia, the Dixon place in Smith County (originally on the Sumner County, North Carolina frontier) is an example of this. Once a county was organized, a structure was needed with at least four rooms for offices (for the register, trustee, county court clerk and sheriff) and a courtroom in which the justices of the peace could meet, either monthly when they performed their judicial functions or quarterly when they acted as the county legislative body, and in which state judges riding circuit could hold court.

As the state grew larger and society and government became more complex, courthouses also grew larger. The increase of personnel in the various offices required more space, and as the county court evolved into the probate court, juvenile court, general sessions court and other courts, the increase in judges, clerks and other personnel led to demands for additional space. The impact on the county courthouse was that in most counties new, larger structures were eventually constructed to contain all of the required offices and functions. In several counties the answer to the space dilemma was to move some functions to an "annex" building. However, it was the practice very early on for the sheriff and the jail to have a structure separate from the courthouse. The jail was only rarely housed in the courthouse; in a few cases additions were constructed to courthouses for this purpose.

Within the counties, towns and cities can be chartered, giving them the power to govern themselves in local matters. Prior to 1953, local or private acts of the state legislature could grant or change charters of towns and cities. Further changes to the older forms of county government include "home rule" and a "metropolitan" form of government. "Home rule" freed incorporated cities from the need to have the legislature pass amendments to their charters. Taking advantage of various city and county functions being combined as a single operation, "metropolitan" government enabled a more efficient and overall less costly form of governing. To date, this type of county structure has been accomplished in Nashville/ Davidson County and Lynchburg/Moore County.

The County Courthouse

With the establishment of a county, the initial courts were often dealing with the selection of a town as the county seat and the planning of a courthouse building. Because of its central administrative and judicial focus, the courthouse quickly became an integral part of the community. Often it was the only central meeting place, apart from churches, and it frequently became the focus of celebrations, emergencies, sometimes religious services, dances, and Masonic gatherings--all in addition to its primary function for the governing of the county and the dispensation of justice.

Because the courthouse was frequently the most interesting and important building in the county and because it was a public building, one with which everyone comes into contact in the course of their lives, it often became a standard for comparison with the next county. However, in Tennessee the courthouse design was usually a more local expression, relating to local values rather than more formalized architectural concerns. As a result, many of the county courthouses in the state were, and continue to be rather modest structures.

The Courthouse Square

One of the most important social and public spaces created in small town planning was a public square around which the town's commercial district usually developed. The very primary role of the courthouse in the county and county seat was usually physically emphasized by a central position in the county seat and the most typical location was in the public square in the middle of the downtown area. As court days were often times of great activity in towns, the status of being the county seat was an often hotly contested and desired prize as it became generator of greater commercial activity.

A view of the Sumner County public square during the Deering dealers Field Day display.

The courthouse square had several planning variations. The most imposing plan, showing off the courthouse to great advantage, is the courthouse square on axis with the major cross streets. Traffic moves into the square at the center of each side and then around the square. This plan is found in Lawrenceburg (Lawrence) and Franklin (Williamson). Probably the best surviving example of this variation, complete with courthouse, is Columbia (Maury). The second variation found the square positioned so that it only interrupted one major street and was flanked by a pair of streets passing by the square in the opposite direction. This plan is used in Brownsville (Haywood) and Murfreesboro (Rutherford).

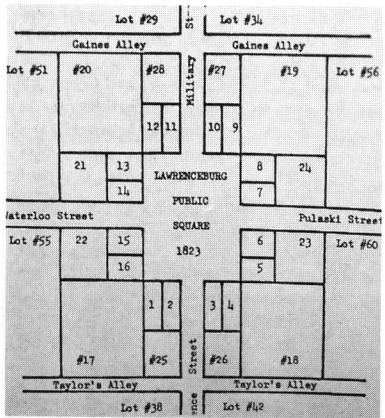

Top: The Lawrenceburg Public Square in 1823. Bottom: The Brownsville Public Square.

The third planning variation finds the courthouse square bordered by pairs of continuous cross streets. Examples here include Fayetteville (Lincoln) and Dyersburg (Dyer). The final variation consists of the courthouse square situated along one or at the corner of two major streets. Jonesborough (Washington) is an example of the former, while Jasper (Marion) and Dandridge (Jefferson) are examples of the latter.

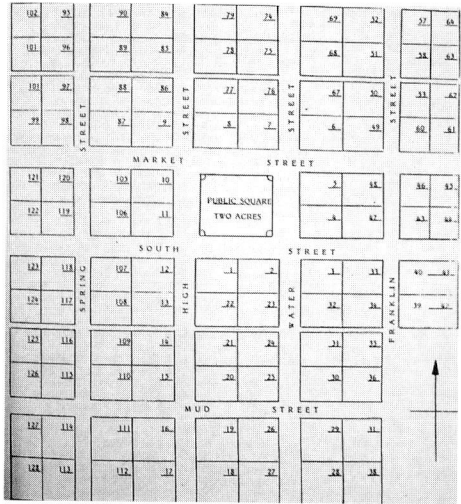

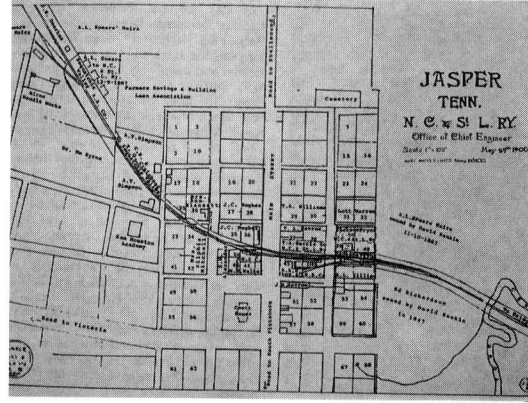

Top: Fayetteville Public Square (1810). Bottom: Jasper Public Square and courthouse (1900).

These planning forms have given way to changes over the decades. Several counties have moved their courthouse out of the public square, either to one side of the square as was done very early in Franklin (Williamson) or completely out of downtown in Lawrenceburg (Lawrence) and Lebanon (Wilson).

Building Materials In Early Courthouses

The initial county court functions during the first year or two of a county's formation often took place in the homes of prominent citizens until such time as the county seat could be set and a courthouse built. The first structure was often temporary in nature and was likely to be built of log. It contained a courtroom and occasionally one or two small rooms used as offices for the judge and court clerk. Over 60 log courthouses are known to have been built in 56 counties. The earliest log courthouse documented was constructed in Washington County in 1778 (while part of North Carolina) and the last in Cheatham County in 1856. One of these log structures, built in 1824 in Hardeman County, was said to be a two story log building.

The combination of readily accessible materials, simple construction technology and low cost made these log structures very popular. Indeed, this was the primary building form in most early communities, derived from the basic vernacular residential building forms of the period. No log courthouses are known to have survived. These small log courthouses will be the most difficult to physically document because they are mentioned generally in brief written accounts surviving in early county records and histories.

With increasing population and development in various areas of the young state, construction methods grew to include heavy timber frame, masonry, and more modern light timber construction. Many of the earliest wood frame and brick courthouses are also based on vernacular residential building types. However, architectural influences from the Eastern seaboard states (Virginia, North Carolina, etc.) began to be felt in the design of more substantial and architecturally evolved designs that presented a character differing from residential buildings.

Only 24 courthouses are known to have been built of wood. The earliest wood frame courthouse was constructed in Grainger County c1801. Over a century later, in 1905, Lake County built the last wood frame courthouse. While less expensive, wood was probably not favored for permanent use because of the increased danger from fire (Lake County's courthouse was enclosed in a brick veneer in 1936). Very few of the early wood courthouses have been visually documented and many were probably meant as temporary structures. Of those documented, all are very simple designs.

The wood frame c1879 Scott County Courthouse.

Stone was a less popular building material, probably due to its greater expense. Only six courthouses were known to have been constructed in stone by 1906, the earliest being in Knox (1797), Campbell (1809) and Anderson Counties (1830). Cumberland County completed two stone courthouses, both of which survive (1886, 1905). Fentress County completed its current stone courthouse in 1906.

Cumberland County's second courthouse (1886) built from local sandstone.

While it was frequently used for trim in a brick structures, stone became a principal building material with the advent of Beaux Arts Neo-Classicism in the early 20th century (Hamilton, and Shelby Counties) and the Art Deco and severe Neo-classicism of the WPA years (Carroll, Davidson, Franklin and Sumner Counties). Only one county, Bledsoe, is known to have constructed a courthouse in concrete (c1900), but it burned a few years after it was finished.

The single most popular building material used in the construction of courthouses proved to be brick. As soon as it became readily available, brick quickly became a primary building material for courthouses. The earliest documented brick courthouse was constructed in the 1790s in Jefferson County. This was followed by courthouses in Jackson (c1806), Williamson (1809), Dickson (c1810), and Maury (1811). Generally described as being square and two story, little other written or graphic evidence survives to conclusively document most of these pre-Civil War brick courthouses. The earliest surviving brick courthouse is the rebuilt c1810 courthouse in Dickson County (1831; this remains the oldest courthouse still in use).

These early brick courthouses continued to differ little from the vernacular residential forms of the period. However, because of the versatility of brick, designs for courthouses prior to the Civil War began to be constructed in many of the better known architectural styles popular in the mid-19th century. Scant documentation indicates that an unusual octagonal two story courthouse was completed in Carter County in 1820.

The 1812 Humphreys County courthouse built at Reynoldsburg.

Stylistic Developments in Courthouse Design

As courthouse designs continued to evolve over time, from small log structures to imposing high-style buildings filled with increasingly complex county functions, this evolution demonstrated the transition of the county seat from a settlement to a judicial and administrative center. The most important role of the courthouse was, and continues to be, that of the county's administrative center and house of justice. Until the post-Civil War period, most courthouses had few functions other than as places for the courts to sit, basic official offices and as archives for county records and exterior designs often reflected this simple functional need.

It was not until the middle decades of the 19th century that Tennessee's county courthouses began to differ markedly from residential architecture. Several early variations proved popular. One was the "four-square" plan ("A", below) which was basically square in form and were generally two stories with a hipped roof and sometimes a cupola. One floor generally contained the courtroom, while the other contained four offices. There was no definite rule for which floor should contain which functions. Examples of this courthouse type include those built for Humphreys (1812), Dickson (1831), Benton (1855), Van Buren (1855) and Clay (1872).

Another popular two story structure was rectangular, usually with a gable roof and sometimes a cupola. On the long side this structure generally featured a recessed portico. The "progenitor" of this type appears to be the 1842 Knox County courthouse, its design repeated in

Type "A" is the simple four-square style. Type "B" represents the simple style popularized by the 1842 Knox County Courthouse. Type "C" is a more complex variety that became increasingly popular for larger courthouses and had a variety of roof configurations.

with some variation in Jefferson (1845), Washington (1847), Grainger (1848), Carter (1852), and Hickman (1867). Major detailing variations included center cupola and gable end designs. This form, with a fully developed projecting center pedimented portico, was used in the Greek Revival Williamson County courthouse in 1859 and an 1858 Warren County structure. Both forms continue to be versions of residential building types of the period.

The Washington County courthouse (1847) modelled after the earlier Knox County courthouse.

Only one example of the New England style meetinghouse design is known to have been constructed. The 1836) Hawkins County courthouse was designed by John Dameron (also designer/builder of the 1825 courthouse in Sullivan County, for which no description survives). This style incorporates the full classical temple front popular in Greek Revival designs with a prominent tower over the front entrance.

Architectural Design: High Style and Designers

The use of early builder/architects in Tennessee has not been well documented. The few known are provincial in their styling, not being trained in the rules of classical architecture. But they often had available to them simple pattern books from which they could develop their designs. Names that have survived connected to courthouses include Thomas Crutchfield (who is said to have completed eight courthouses), Joseph Coe, William Seawell, Benjamin Gholson and Micajah and William McElroy.

The 1836 Hawkins County courthouse.

By the 1840s and 50s Greek Revival style structures began to appear. While this eventually became a predominant local style, it was not used in many courthouses. One of the earliest examples was in Greene County (1823). Other important examples include those constructed in

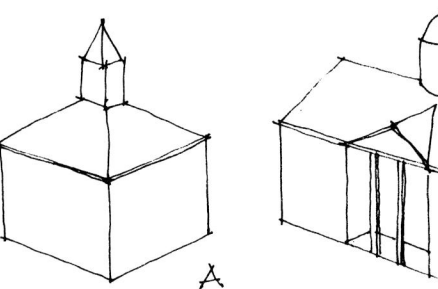 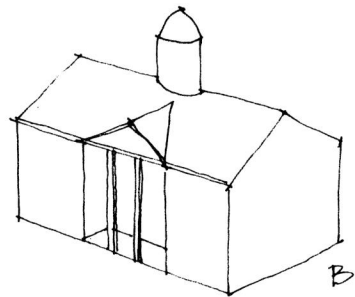 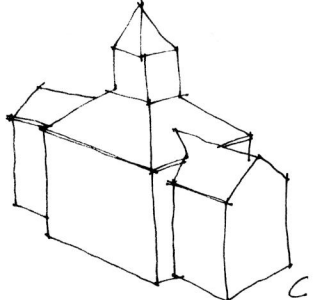

Sumner (1837), Maury (1846), Wilson (1848) and Davidson (1857, both designed by William Strickland), Roane (1856) and Rutherford (1859). These designs range from simple attached two and three story pilasters and full entablatures at roof level to fully developed classical temple porticoes.

Top: A late example is seen in the simple Greek Revival styling of the 1867 Dyer County courthouse. Bottom: The 1856 Roane County courthouse featured fully developed classical porticoes and an unusual three story office configuration on one side.

The Civil War Years: 1861-1865

Despite the many battles and lengthy Union occupation, the Civil War did not take a heavy toll on Tennessee's county courthouses. Of the 21 counties whose courthouses were impacted by both sides during the war, only 11 were actually burned. Those courthouses destroyed included Bedford (carelessness of Confederate forces), Dyer, Hardeman, Hardin, Henderson (by accident of Union forces), Hickman (to prevent its use by Union forces), Monroe, Perry, Putnam, Stewart and Sullivan. Other courthouses used by both sides or damaged during the war were Benton, Blount, Giles, Lawrence, Macon, Madison, Obion, Rutherford, Washington and Williamson. Uses made of the courthouses included offices, barracks, and hospitals.

Stylistic Evolution: 1865-1939

By the early 1850s, and following the Civil War the South began to respond more creatively to new tastes and interest in alternative architectural styles began to develop. The South began to recover from war in the 1870s and this resulted in increased building activity. Tennessee, however, was still more conservative than its northern counterparts.

The most elaborate structures constructed in Tennessee counties occurred during the last half of the 19th century. Design was often eclectic, using no one particular style, but many details from various styles of this period. This period also saw non-residential building types diverging significantly from residential design, becoming readily distinguishable as building types became increasingly specialized.

The *Italianate* style, with its lower pitched roofs, brackets, wide eaves, and tall, narrow semicircular topped windows (sometimes with elaborate hoods), and cupolas and towers were incorporated into a number of courthouse designs. (Similar Italianate details were also added to earlier buildings in "stylistic" updatings.)

The Italianate 1868 Hardeman County courthouse.

As courthouses grew in function and size, courthouse designs became increasingly elaborate, frequently incorporating projecting corner and center pavilions, towers, bays, richer trim and detailing and complex roof forms. These more complex designs were not only more interesting, but they established a strong presence on their respective public squares.

During the late 1860s the Second Empire of Napoleon III's Paris was well established in

The Second Empire Smith County courthouse (1877).

United States. The *Second Empire* style is readily identifiable its use of various shaped mansard roofs and towers and for its horizontal layering and projecting pavilions in the center and at corners of the building. This style became popular for governmental buildings throughout the country and included courthouses in Franklin, Hamilton, Robertson and Smith Counties.

Simple Neo-classical detailing is combined with complex massing in the 1897 Monroe County courthouse.

The architectural profession had fully developed in Tennessee and a number of firms both in and out of the state were even specializing in courthouse designs. Several had developed standard packages to which they could add exterior stylistic variations to suit the client. Best known for courthouse designs during the late 19th and early 20th centuries were the Tennessee firms of Bauman and Bauman (Knoxville, 5 courthouses), A.C. Bruce (Nashville/Knoxville, 4 courthouses), William Chamberlain & Co. (Knoxville, 6 courthouses) and R.M. Hunt (Chattanooga, 7 courthouses).

From out of state also came noted courthouse designers such as the McDonald Brothers from Louisville (Sevier and Tipton County courthouses) and S.W. Bunting of Indianapolis (Montgomery County courthouse). Both firms had developed practices that specialized in courthouse designs and these standard designs, sometimes with little revision, appeared in many states.

The more eclectic Victorian Anderson County courthouse (1890) demonstrates richly decorated walls combined with towers and a complex roof.

By the late 19th century architectural training had become more formalized and the rising star was the *Beaux Arts* classicism developed in Europe. This style was an exceptionally strong influence on the design of the buildings for the World Columbian Exposition in Chicago in 1894. This fair's classical designs spread interest in this style far and wide. What the public saw was a monumental classicism, with its carefully developed use of the Greek and Roman orders lavishly applied to public buildings. (In residential structures it was not uncommon to be simplified without columns). By using this style, architects could design courthouses in such a way that even a small courthouse could dominate a town's public square. The materials used often ranged from brick, to stone, to stucco, to wood.

Top: The Beaux Arts Maury County courthouse (1906). Bottom: The Classical Revival 1912 Washington County courthouse.

After 1900 the situation continued to change as courthouses grew larger everywhere as country business increased. They continued to be designed primarily as monumental buildings and public monuments and not merely as office buildings, although this emphasis was also shifting.

Architects began to give up on the strict interpretation of the classical orders, substituting a more abstract treatment of wall surfaces. This was soon combined together with influences borrowed from the 1925 Paris world's fair and its *Art Deco* style. These components continued to be used through the Works Progress Administration public architecture of the Depression-era. Scraped classical designs with Art Deco touches almost became the official WPA style.

Top: The Art Deco inspired design of the Lauderdale County courthouse (1936). Bottom: the 1940 severely classical Sumner County courthouse. Both designs, by the Nashville architectural firm of Marr & Holman, demonstrate their high level of skill and stylistic range.

The Evolution of the Courthouse into Modern Times

Following World War II, courthouse design becomes generally uninspired, with architectural design following on the functional theories which abandoned historic styles and detailing that were developing in the 1930s and 40s. The buildings constructed are often basically functional designs that conceive of the courthouse more as an office building and rarely as a monumental public structure. Also, after the war, the cost of materials escalated and a change in attitude occurred. There was no longer a will to utilize fine materials and craftsmanship as cost becomes an increasing factor. As a result, few of our "modern" courthouses have achieved the character and monumental public feeling or retain the social and community aspects of the pre-war courthouses.

While no courthouses were built during World War II, twenty-three have since been completed. The most recent is the Grundy County courthouse, completed in 1996 and replacing the old Victorian structure destroyed by arson several years ago. Courthouses have continued to increase in size because of increasing needs for office space, in additional to the judicial functions. The designs completed have ranged considerably in terms of composition and materials.

There was also a perceived, but not necessarily actual need to move the county courthouse from the public square to a peripheral location away from downtown because of space and parking needs. To some extent this has also resulted in the decline in the social function of the courthouse and the loss of the individualism of 19th century.

The 1979 Knox City-County Annex building constructed near the old county courthouse in Knoxville is a handsome addition to the city's riverside.

Those counties which have preserved their older courthouses in favor of constructing (or renovating) buildings as courthouse annex facilities have generally retained the cherished social functions played by the courthouse without sacrificing the quality of their public services.

Contents - Alphabetical by County

County	County Seat	Page
Anderson	Clinton	2
Bedford	Shelbyville	4
Benton	Camden	6
Bledsoe	Pikeville	8
Blount	Maryville	10
Bradley	Cleveland	12
Campbell	Jacksboro	14
Cannon	Woodbury	16
Carroll	Huntington	18
Carter	Elizabethton	20
Cheatham	Ashland City	22
Chester	Henderson	24
Claiborne	Tazewell	26
Clay	Celina	28
Cocke	Newport	30
Coffee	Manchester	32
Crockett	Alamo	34
Cumberland	Crossville	36
Davidson	Nashville	38
Decatur	Decaturville	40
Dekalb	Smithville	42
Dickson	Charlotte	44
Dyer	Dyersburg	46
Fayette	Sommerville	48
Fentress	Jamestown	50
Franklin	Winchester	52
Gibson	Trenton	54
Giles	Pulaski	56
Grainger	Rutledge	58
Greene	Greeneville	60
Grundy	Altamont	62
Hamblen	Morristown	64
Hamilton	Chattanooga	66
Hancock	Sneedville	68

County	County Seat	Page
Hardeman	Bolivar	70
Hardin	Savannah	72
Hawkins	Rogersville	74
Haywood	Brownsville	76
Henderson	Lexington	78
Henry	Paris	80
Hickman	Centerville	82
Houston	Erin	84
Humphreys	Waverly	86
Jackson	Gainesboro	88
James	*Ooltewah*	192
Jefferson	Dandridge	90
Johnson	Mountain City	92
Knox	Knoxville	94
Lake	Tiptonville	96
Lauderdale	Ripley	98
Lawrence	Lawrenceburg	100
Lewis	Hohenwald	102
Lincoln	Fayetteville	104
Loudon	Loudon	106
Macon	Lafayette	108
Madison	Jackson	110
Marion	Jasper	112
Marshall	Lewisburg	114
Maury	Columbia	116
McMinn	Athens	118
McNairy	Selmer	120
Meigs	Decatur	122
Monroe	Madisonville	124
Montgomery	Clarksville	126
Moore	Lynchburg	128
Morgan	Wartburg	130
Obion	Union City	132
Overton	Livingston	134

County	County Seat	Page
Perry	Linden	136
Pickett	Byrdstown	138
Polk	Benton	140
Putnam	Cookville	142
Rhea	Dayton	144
Roane	Kingston	146
Robertson	Springfield	148
Rutherford	Murfreesboro	150
Scott	Huntsville	152
Sequatchie	Dunlap	154
Sevier	Sevierville	156
Shelby	Memphis	158
Smith	Carthage	160
Stewart	Dover	162
Sullivan	Blountville	164
Sumner	Gallatin	166
Tennessee	*Clarksville*	193
Tipton	Covington	168
Trousdale	Hartsville	170
Unicoi	Erwin	172
Union	Maynardsville	174
Van Buren	Spencer	176
Warren	McMinnville	178
Washington	Jonesboro	180
Wayne	Waynesboro	182
Weakley	Dresden	184
White	Sparta	186
Williamson	Franklin	188
Wilson	Lebanon	190

Dates of County Formation		194
Notes		195
Photo Credits		198
Bibliography		201

Contents - Alphabetical by County Seat

County Seat	County	Page
Alamo	Crockett	34
Altamont	Grundy	62
Ashland City	Cheatham	22
Athens	McMinn	118
Benton	Polk	140
Blountville	Sullivan	164
Bolivar	Hardeman	68
Brownsville	Haywood	76
Byrdstown	Pickett	138
Camden	Benton	6
Carthage	Smith	160
Celina	Clay	28
Centerville	Hickman	82
Charlotte	Dickson	44
Chattanooga	Hamilton	66
Clarksville	Montgomery	128
Clarksville	*Tennessee*	193
Cleveland	Bradley	12
Clinton	Anderson	2
Columbia	Maury	116
Cookville	Putnam	142
Covington	Tipton	168
Crossville	Cumberland	36
Dandridge	Jefferson	90
Dayton	Rhea	144
Decatur	Meigs	122
Decaturville	Decatur	40
Dover	Stewart	162
Dresden	Weakley	184
Dunlap	Sequatchie	154
Dyersburg	Dyer	46
Elizabethton	Carter	20
Erin	Houston	84
Erwin	Unicoi	172
Fayetteville	Lincoln	104
Franklin	Williamson	188
Gallatin	Sumner	166
Gainesboro	Jackson	88
Greeneville	Greene	60
Hartsville	Trousdale	170
Henderson	Chester	24
Hohenwald	Lewis	102
Huntington	Carroll	18
Huntsville	Scott	152
Jacksboro	Campbell	14
Jackson	Madison	110
Jamestown	Fentress	50
Jasper	Marion	112
Jonesboro	Washington	180
Kingston	Roane	146
Knoxville	Knox	94
Lafayette	Macon	108
Lawrenceburg	Lawrence	100
Lebanon	Wilson	190
Lewisburg	Marshall	114
Lexington	Henderson	78
Linden	Perry	136
Livingston	Overton	134
Loudon	Loudon	106
Lynchburg	Moore	128
Madisonville	Monroe	124
Manchester	Coffee	32
Maryville	Blount	10
Maynardsville	Union	174
McMinnville	Warren	178
Memphis	Shelby	158
Morristown	Hamblen	64
Mountain City	Johnson	92
Murfreesboro	Rutherford	150
Nashville	Davidson	38
Newport	Cocke	30
Ooltewah	*James*	192
Paris	Henry	80
Pikeville	Bledsoe	8
Pulaski	Giles	56
Ripley	Lauderdale	98
Rogersville	Hawkins	74
Rutledge	Grainger	58
Savannah	Hardin	72
Selmer	McNairy	120
Sevierville	Sevier	156
Shelbyville	Bedford	4
Smithville	Dekalb	42
Sneedville	Hancock	68
Sommerville	Fayette	48
Sparta	White	186
Spencer	Van Buren	176
Springfield	Robertson	148
Tazewell	Claiborne	26
Tiptonville	Lake	96
Trenton	Gibson	54
Union City	Obion	132
Wartburg	Morgan	130
Waverley	Humphreys	86
Waynesboro	Wayne	182
Winchester	Franklin	52
Woodbury	Cannon	16

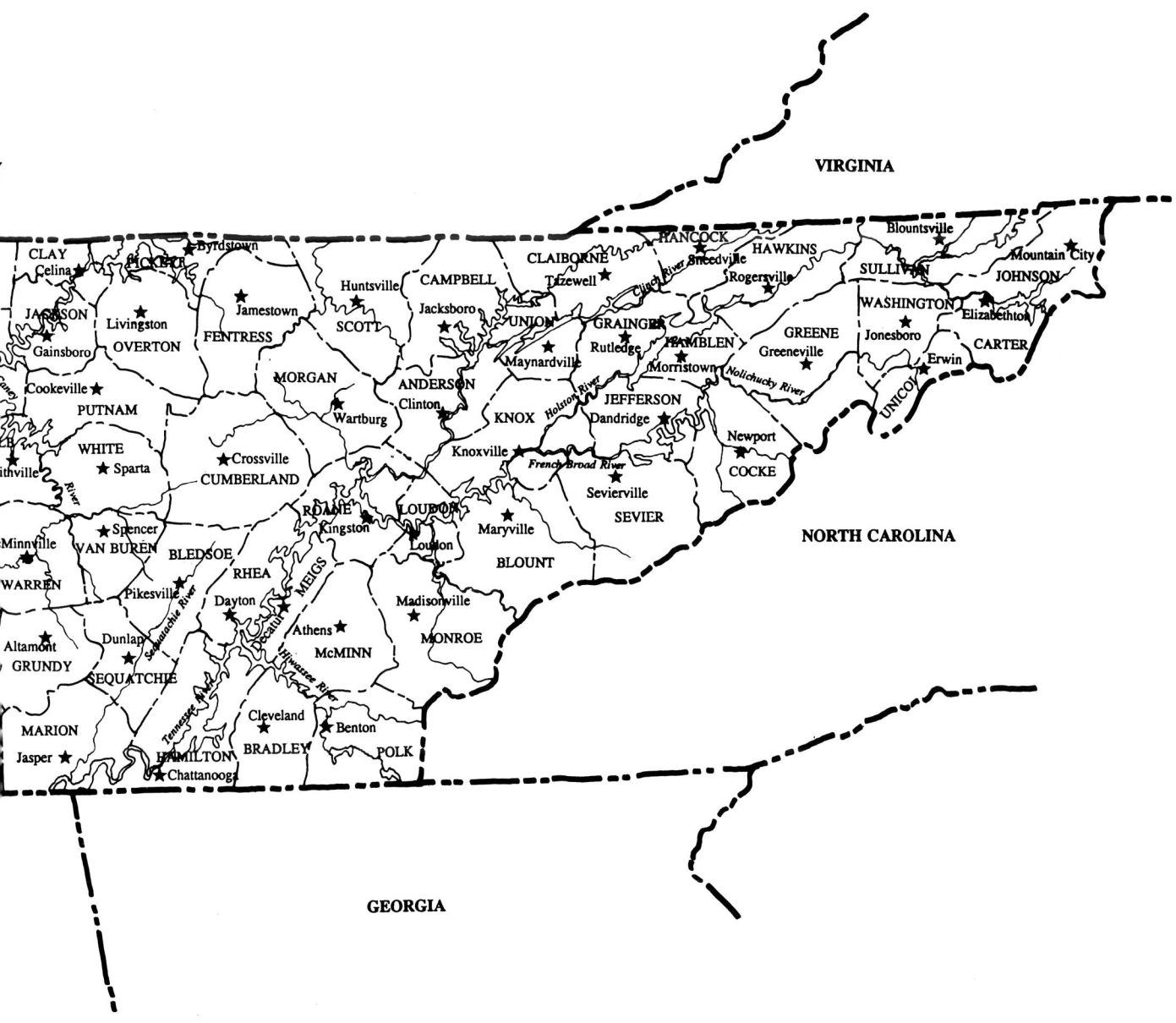

TENNESSEE and its STATE CAPITOLS

On the Way to Statehood

Following the close of the American Revolution in 1783, many settlers flocked into the Tennessee country, then part of the state of North Carolina. Congress had attempted to persuade the eastern states to give their western lands to the United States. While some did, North Carolina thought about it, but decided not to do so. As part of its plan, Congress encouraged settlers west of the mountains to begin thinking about forming new states.

Leaders of the eastern Tennessee settlements decided to form a new state. In 1784 representatives of Greene, Washington and Sullivan counties held meetings at Jonesborough and declared themselves independent of North Carolina. John Sevier was elected governor of the new State of Franklin (named for Benjamin Franklin) and a constitution was adopted. Congress did not recognize the new state and the North Carolina legislature refused to both give up the western country or to give the settlers independence. The movement for a separate state of Franklin eventually collapsed. In 1790 North Carolina finally ceded the western lands to the United States and Congress immediately organized it into the Southwest Territory (Territory South of the River Ohio). William Blount was appointed governor, moving to Knoxville in 1792.

1784: Capitol of the State of Franklin, Greeneville.

1790: Capitol of the Southwest Territory, Rocky Mount.

The Southwest Territory was made up of two districts: the eastern Washington District (Washington, Greene, Sullivan and Hawkins counties) and the Mero District of Middle Tennessee (Davidson, Sumner and Tennessee counties). Indian troubles filled the short life of the territory. Finally, the Pickney Treaty of 1795 between the United States and Spain stopped the Spaniards from stirring up the Indians and the US gave the Cherokees more money for the lands they had given up by the Treaty of Holston in 1791.

In 1795 the territorial legislature ordered a census and held a vote on whether or not the people wished to become a state in the Union. The vote was in favor of statehood and a constitutional convention was held in Knoxville on January 11, 1796. The new state was to be called Tennessee and the Middle Tennessee county bearing this name gave it up and was divided into the new counties of Montgomery and Robertson. John Sevier was elected governor. There was, however, some delay in Congress, and Tennessee became the sixteenth state in the Union on June 1, 1796.

1792: Capitol of the Southwest Territory, Blount Mansion, Knoxville.

Tennessee's Capital Cities

It took nearly half a century following statehood (June 1, 1796) before Tennessee could decide upon a permanent capital for its government. While many cities were promoted, suggested or quarreled over, four towns actually served as the seat of state government - one of them for only one day.

Following Tennessee's entry into the union in 1796, the state constitution provided that the state's largest city would serve as the seat of government until 1802. Knoxville, the former governmental seat of the Territory South of the River Ohio and the largest city in the new state thus continued in its role as the capital. Subsequent legislative acts kept the capital in Knoxville for an additional four years.

1796: First Capitol of Tennessee, Knoxville.

A one day session of the General Assembly was held in Kingston in 1807. One of the two resolutions passed moved the capital back to Knoxville the next day and Knoxville remained the capital for an additional five years.

1807: Second Capitol of Tennessee, Kingston.

Increasing population in the Middle Tennessee grand division resulted in Nashville becoming the capital in 1812. However, attempts to relocate the capital began immediately, with the result being a move back to Knoxville in 1815.

Knoxville's role as capital city ended in 1817 with the designation of Murfreesboro as the seat of government. This lasted until 1826, when the capital was again moved to Nashville. The Constitutional Convention of 1834, while not choosing a permanent capital city, delegated that responsibility to the General Assembly meeting in 1843.

At this time efforts were being made to locate the capital in the geographical center of the state, which was determined to be about one and one-half miles east of Murfreesboro in Rutherford County. Cities being promoted, in addition to Nashville, included Carrollsville, McMinnville, Murfreesboro, Carthage, Middletown and Clarksville.

Though the Convention did not name a permanent capital, it did have a responsibility for providing for an interim seat of government. Again both Nashville and Murfreesboro were promoted, in addition to Franklin and Columbia. The Convention adjourned after determining that Nashville would continue as capital under the first two legislatures under the new constitution. Again, despite much discussion, Nashville continued to serve as capital until 1843.

The spirited battle over the capital issue came to an end in the 1843 legislative session. Many cities were again proposed and one unusual proposal included a biennial shift between Knoxville and Jackson, with extraordinary sessions being held in Carthage. With most of the cities being voted down, the Senate selected Kingston while the

1812: Third Capitol of Tennessee, Nashville.

House picked Murfreesboro. The House refused to accept Kingston but did not insist on Murfreesboro, while the Senate did not insist on Kingston, but voted against Murfreesboro, Clarksville and Columbia. Finally, on October 7, 1843, both houses concurred on Nashville and the bitter fight was over.

Once the decision was made, it became necessary to construct a capitol building. Prior to 1843, while Nashville had been the capital, the legislature met in a building on Broadway (where Hume-Fogg High School is now located. Cedar Knob, the highest point in Nashville, was purchased for $30,000 from Judge George W. Campbell and William Strickland, one of the most prominent architects in the country at that time, was selected to design and supervise the construction of a new capitol building. While the building was under construction, the legislature met in the Masonic Hall.

The State Capitol Building

The cornerstone for the new capitol was laid on July 4, 1845 and the final stone put in place on July 21, 1855. The General Assembly first met in the new capitol building on October 3, 1853, prior to the completion of the structure.

Completed in 1859, the Tennessee State Capitol building is considered a masterpiece of Greek Revival architecture. Designed by architect William Strickland of Philadelphia, the building was completed following his death under the supervision of his son Francis.

The building is constructed of Tennessee limestone and the labor was provided by slaves and convicts. Covering an area 112 by 239 feet, it rises to a height of 206 feet, 7 inches from the ground to the top of its tower. The building follows the plan of an Ionic temple. It has pedimented porticoes consisting of eight columns on the north and south facades, with six column

The State Capitol Building under nearly complete, c1860.

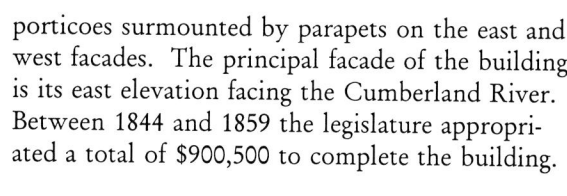

The Capitol grounds occupied by Union troops.

porticoes surmounted by parapets on the east and west facades. The principal facade of the building is its east elevation facing the Cumberland River. Between 1844 and 1859 the legislature appropriated a total of $900,500 to complete the building.

In 1862 the building was placed under heavy guard by Union forces, surrounded by a blockade and was renamed Fort Johnson (for Andrew Johnson, the military governor of Tennessee.) Governor Isham G. Harris had moved the seat of government and the archives to Memphis during this period.

At his request William Strickland was buried in the northeast corner of the capitol's walls. Also buried in the walls of the capitol, at the southeast corner is Samuel D. Morgan, the president of the capitol commission, with whom Strickland often argued over project funding. President James K.

Polk and his wife Sarah Childress Polk are also buried on the capitol grounds.

Capitol Building Renovations

The General Assembly provided funds for the exterior renovation of the capitol building in 1953, followed by a 1957 appropriation for the interior renovation. Exterior work begun in 1956 and included some 90,000 cubic feet of Indiana limestone, used to replace the columns, capitals, pediments and other decorative elements that had severely deteriorated. New windows and a new copper roof were installed at this time as well.

Interior restoration work, begun in 1958 included the excavation and finishing out of the crypt for additional office space and legislative committee rooms. Also completed were a new electrical system, heating and air conditioning and plaster restoration. New corridor floors of Missouri Carthage marble were also installed. In 1959 the Motlow Tunnel and two elevators were added to the project.

Above: Wood engraving of the Capitol by H. Bosse, 1860, showing the early capitol grounds. Below: A 1911 view of the Capitol with views of the Capitol Annex and the old Governor's Mansion purchased from J.A. Gray.

Renovation work in 1969-70 included the renovation of the Senate and House chambers, committee rooms and second floor offices. A second exterior facelift in 1985 involved cleaning the stone as well as the selective repair and replacement of deteriorated stonework. At that time a Capitol Restoration Committee was established and an historic structures report was completed.

In 1986 the State Capitol Committee was created to develop a master plan to guide the continuing restoration of the building. Completed in 1987 was the restoration of the original Legislative Library, followed by the restoration of the first floor and portions of the second floor, completed in 1988. Included were the restoration of the

Used as state offices, the Capitol Annex was formerly the residence of Bishop Byrne.

original state Supreme Court room as well as the offices of the Governor, his staff and those of the constitutional officers.

Bicentennial Capitol Mall

The centennial of Tennessee's statehood in 1896 resulted in the Centennial Exposition of 1897, now remembered as Centennial Park in Nashville and the rebuilt Parthenon from the exposition. Now as part of Tennessee's Bicentennial celebration, the state has completed a new Bicentennial Capitol Mall. This mall is intended to permanently preserve the sight-lines of its elegant and persevering Greek Revival capitol building, which has gone from being the dominant feature of Nashville's skyline to a structure viewed amidst a larger, modern city. Today only the northern and western views of the capitol building are unobstructed. Land to the north of the capitol was acquired to create a lasting monument to the state's Bicentennial and, more importantly, to preserve the northward vista of the Capitol building. The mall is a 19-acre outdoor history museum honoring Tennessee's 95 counties as well as commemorating the state's 200-year history. Included are a 2000 seat amphitheater, fountains and extensive landscaping.

Top left: General plan of the 1996 Bicentennial Mall area showing the state capital building (bottom center), new farmers market complex (upper left) and parking (upper right). Bottom left: General view of the granite map of the state, new railroad trestle, rivers of Tennessee area and amphitheater. Right: An enlarged plan of the actual mall area.

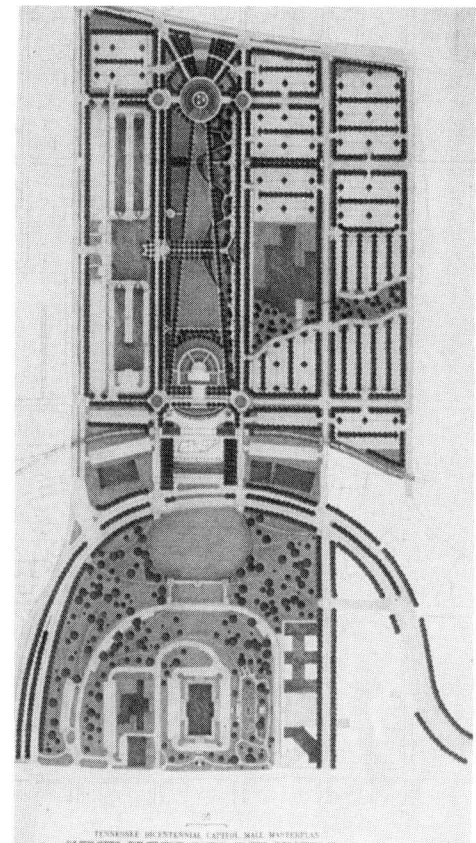
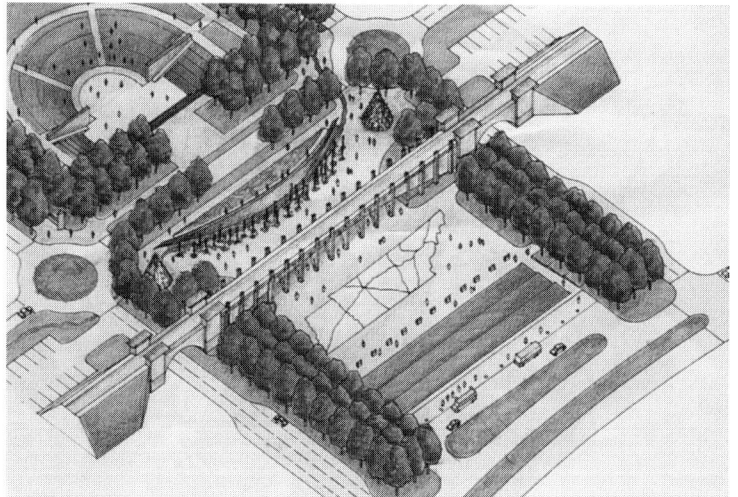
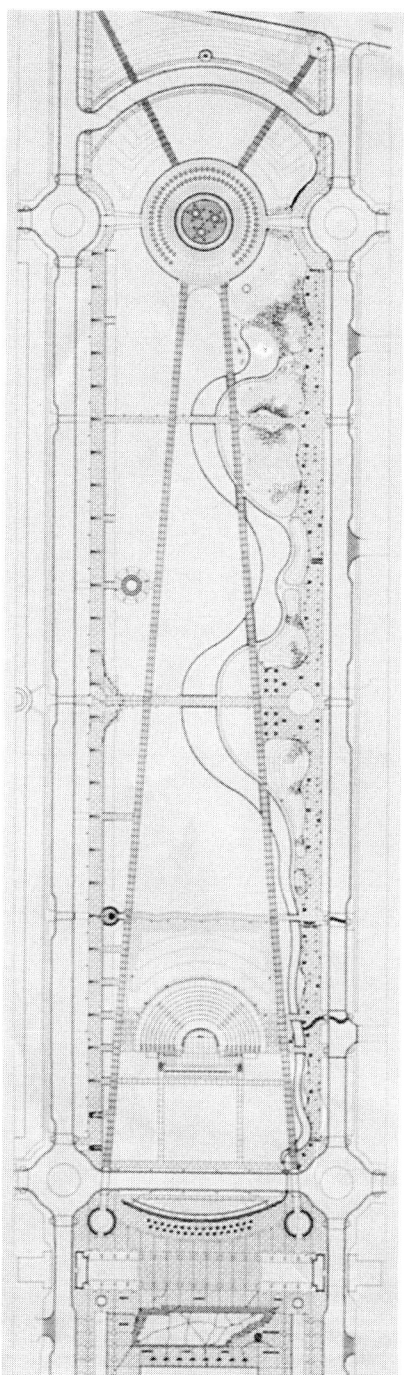

ANDERSON COUNTY

Formed: December 13, 1801
Formed from: Knox County
County seat: Clinton
Area: 338 sq.mi.

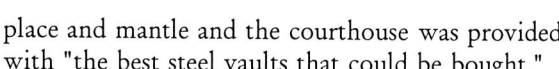

Anderson County was named after Joseph Anderson, a United States senator and judge for the Territory South of the Ohio River. The county seat was originally named Burrville after Aaron Burr who was, at that time, Vice President of the United States. It was renamed Clinton on Nov. 8, 1809 to honor DeWitt Clinton, a sponsor of the Erie Canal and governor of New York.[1]

The first court met in 1801 at the log residence of Joseph Denham in Eagle Bend. At that time the first courthouse, a log structure completed in 1803, was planned. The second court was held at the home of John Leib until the completion of the courthouse.[2] Two acres were reserved near the center of the town for the courthouse, prison, and stocks. This was to be paid for by the sale of town lots.

The second courthouse, a two-story rough stone structure with an outside stairway and a log jail at rear was completed in 1830. It was constructed close to site of original courthouse.

This courthouse was replaced in 1889-90 by a third structure designed in the high Victorian style popular at the time. It was a tall, two story brick courthouse and cost $35,500.[3] In addition to the tall tower with its clocks, this design also featured four shorter square corner towers, large stone trimmed arched windows and doors, and decorative finials and cresting on the towers and main roof.

On the interior there were twin staircases in the front hall and an unusual circular courtroom on the second floor. Each office had its own fireplace and mantle and the courthouse was provided with "the best steel vaults that could be bought."

This courthouse was replaced in 1967 by the current Anderson County courthouse, which was completed at a cost of $1,530,000. Martin J. Lide of Birmingham, Alabama was the architect.[4]

Right: Anderson County's third courthouse. Left: The third courthouse in the process of demolition.

BEDFORD COUNTY

Formed: December 3, 1807
Formed from: Rutherford County
County seat: Shelbyville
Area: 474 sq.mi.

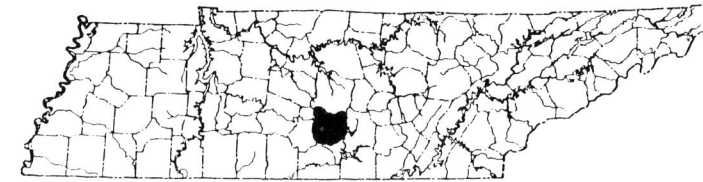

Bedford County was named for Thomas Bedford Jr., an officer in the Revolutionary War. He moved to Tennessee around 1795 and contributed to the development of Rutherford County. The court was organized in the home of Mrs. Payne near the head of Mulberry Creek in 1808. After the county was reduced in size in 1809, a committee was appointed to locate the county seat and selected the home of Amos Balch, two to three miles southeast of Shelbyville as a temporary location. The county seat was permanently established at Shelbyville in 1810 (named for Colonel Isaac Shelby). Shelbyville was incorporated on October 7, 1819.[1]

The first courthouse, of wood frame construction, was completed around 1810 on the northwest corner of the square. It was followed in 1821 by a brick courthouse on the same site, which was destroyed by a tornado in 1830. A third courthouse followed in 1830. This was a large brick structure which was destroyed by a fire in 1863 resulting from carelessness on the part of Confederate soldiers.[2] After the War the courts were held in various places until a new courthouse could be completed.

The county's fourth courthouse, located in the center of the square, was begun in 1869 and was completed in 1873. At the time it was one of the largest and handsomest in the state, costing $120,000. This building was constructed of brick on a blue limestone base. The pillars above the base were cast iron, Corinthian in style. This building was surmounted by a cupola with a clock and bell. It contained a principal courtroom 40 x 90 feet and two additional 20 x 40 foot courtrooms. Including porches, the courthouse was 91' wide and 120 feet long. The courthouse also burned, this time by a lynch mob in 1934.[3]

The current, fifth courthouse, was completed in 1935. Designed by Marr and Holman, Architects of Nashville, it basically duplicates the design of the fourth courthouse. However, small design changes were made in the new structure, including the elimination of the decorative brackets around the entablature and an altered design for the top of the cupola. Sufficient brick was salvaged from its predecessor to face the new building.

The fourth courthouse had arched windows on the ground floor and decorative finials and cresting at the top of the cupola.

BENTON COUNTY

Formed: November 24, 1835
Formed from: Henry and Humphreys Counties
County Seat: Camden
Area: 394 sq. miles

Benton County, originally named for Thomas Hart Benton, was renamed for David Benton, an early settler, pioneer magistrate, and veteran of the War of 1812. The county courts were organized in 1836 and initially met at the house of Samuel Haliburton in Tranquility. Here was built the first courthouse, called the "jury room." It was constructed of plain logs and was 18 x 20 feet, costing $22.50.[1]

With the move of the county seat to Camden in 1837, a two story brick courthouse was completed later that year. Built by Samuel Ingram for $3,270.18, this structure was 30 x 36 feet and contained county offices on first floor and a courtroom on second. This, and all subsequent courthouses were constructed in the middle of the public square, a half acre of ground enclosed by a rail fence.

The second courthouse was demolished by Col. Irvin B. Carns, who was contracted to build a new courthouse for $5,598.75 in 1855. After some controversy as to whether a frame or brick building should be built, the decision was made to use brick for the 30 x 40 foot two story courthouse.[2] Its interior arrangements were similar to those of the previous building. It served as temporary headquarters for federal soldiers during the Civil War, and was repaired in 1867. It was later declared unsafe and was demolished.

The fourth courthouse was completed in 1877. It was a large, two story structure. Set on a stone foundation, it was constructed of brick, had long narrow windows, and was topped with a cupola. The roof, on the verge of collapse in 1891, was repaired.

A new courthouse was authorized in 1915, resulting in the demolition of the fourth courthouse. This next structure, again a two story brick building, was one of the more ornate courthouses built. It was trimmed with stone and had a taller central section with a second floor courtroom. It was demolished in 1972.

The current courthouse, completed in 1974, is Benton County's sixth. This building was designed by Hart, Freeland and Roberts, Architects of Nashville.

Left: The third courthouse. Right: The fifth courthouse.

BLEDSOE COUNTY

Formed: November 30, 1807
Formed from: Roane County
County seat: Pikeville
Area: 406 sq.mi.

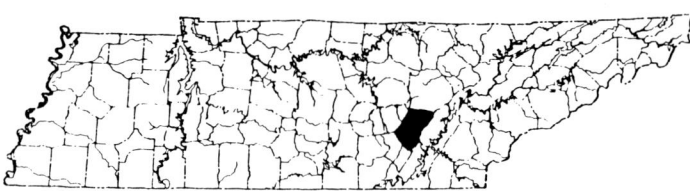

Bledsoe County was named for Anthony Bledsoe, a captain in the Colonial Army of Virginia, major in the Revolutionary War, and colonel in the Tennessee Militia. The first county court met at the home of a Mr. Thomas. A log courthouse, jail, and stocks were soon erected at Old Madison.

Old Madison was succeeded as county seat by Pikeville sometime between the close of the War of 1812 and 1818. It was probably named for Gen. Zebulon Pike, the soldier-explorer for whom Pike's Peak is named.

Pikeville's first courthouse was completed prior to 1821. This was a two story brick structure which, by 1860 was in need of repairs. A new courthouse was constructed in the early 1900s. Built of concrete, this structure burned in December of 1909, resulting in a law suit against the Fall City Construction Company for faulty construction of the flues.[1] The design consisted of a central square block with lower wings to each side. It also had a hipped roof and central cupola.

The current courthouse, Bledsoe County's fourth, was completed in November of 1910 at a cost of $14,693.15 and was designed by the architect W.K. Brown.[2] This is a two story brick structure on a stone foundation. It has a stylized classical projecting entry portico.

Left: View of the third courthouse during the fire which destroyed the building. Right: An early view of Bledsoe County's current courthouse.

BLOUNT COUNTY

Formed: July 11, 1795
Formed from: Knox County
County seat: Maryville
Area: 559 sq.mi.

Blount County was named for William Blount, a member of the Continental Congress, governor of the Territory South of the Ohio River, and a senator from Tennessee. The court of Pleas and Quarter Sessions was organized at the home of Abraham Weaver in September of 1795. The second court term was held at the home of John Craig.

The county seat, Maryville, was named for William Blount's wife, Mary Grainger Blount. It was located on 50 acres originally owned by John Craig. The first attempt at constructing a courthouse in 1799 met with failure. A new commission was established in 1802, and a temporary courthouse of log construction was completed. This courthouse was used until 1820.[1]

A second, wood frame courthouse was erected in 1820 at a cost of $571.33.[2] Josiah Danforth was the contractor for this structure. The design of this structure was unusual in that it had a recessed porch on the first and part of the second floors.

In 1840 a two story brick courthouse was constructed. Basically square in plan, it featured projecting center bays and corner pilasters. This courthouse was damaged during the Civil War during a Confederate attack and burned in 1879.

Architect J.F. Bauman was responsible for the design of the next courthouse, costing $12,779.01.[3] It was also a two story brick structure completed in 1880. The typical Victorian design included a tall, three story mansard roofed tower. It was destroyed by a fire on July 27, 1907.

The current courthouse, built in 1906, is the county's fifth. Of Neo-classical design, it features projecting columned porticos and a tall central clock tower. This structure was designed by Bauman Brothers, Architects and cost $80,000 (including its furnishings).

Left: The second courthouse. Center: The third courthouse. Right: The fourth courthouse completed in 1880.

BRADLEY COUNTY

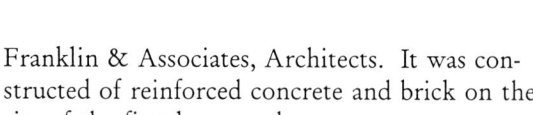

Formed: February 10, 1836
Formed from: Indian lands of southeast Tennessee
County seat: Cleveland
Area: 329 sq.mi.

Bradley County was named for Colonel Edward Bradley of Shelby County, a lieutenant colonel in the 15th Regiment of the Tennessee (Bradley's) Volunteers in War of 1812. The first court sessions were held at McCaslin's Methodist Campground near Chatata Creek. The earliest courthouse was the Cherokee courthouse of the Amohee District, at Thompson Spring.[1]

Cleveland was laid out in 1836 and was selected in 1837 as the county seat. It was named for Col. Benjamin Cleveland of North Carolina, a Revolutionary War hero. The initial courthouse, a log structure, was built near the southwest corner of the courthouse yard.

This was followed in 1840 by a two story brick structure, the first formal courthouse, built by Thomas Crutchfield for $8,000. The exterior design of this courthouse apparently had two story brick pilasters and was topped by a hipped roof and center cupola. It was razed in 1892.

The third courthouse costing $75,000, was designed by Hunt and Lamm, Architects.[2] It was a two story brick structure having a wide arched first floor entry, above which was an open recessed loggia. The design included corner pyramid roofed pavilions and a tall clock tower on its principal elevation. This courthouse remained in use until 1963, when it was demolished to make way for a new structure.

The present courthouse, the county's fourth, was completed in 1964 and was designed by Selmon T. Franklin & Associates, Architects. It was constructed of reinforced concrete and brick on the site of the first log courthouse.

Left: Sketch of the second courthouse. Right: View of the third courthouse in the 1930s.

CAMPBELL COUNTY

Formed: September 11, 1806
Formed from: Anderson and Claiborne Counties
County seat: Jacksboro
Area: 480 sq.mi.

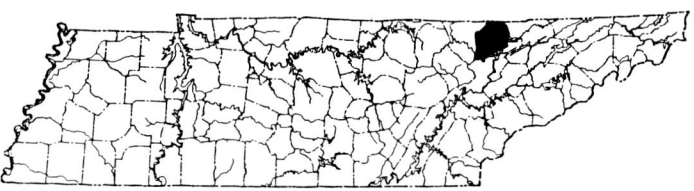

Campbell County was named for Colonel Arthur Campbell, commander of the 70th regiment of the Virginia Militia in Revolutionary War. Campbell was also the Commissioner responsible for negotiating the Indian Treaties of 1781. The initial session of the Court of Pleas and Quarter Sessions was held at the home of Richard Linville in December of 1806.[1]

The county seat, Jacksboro, was laid out in and a stone courthouse and jail were erected in 1808. Jacksborough, as it was originally spelled, was named for Judge John F. Jack of Rutledge, who deeded the 60 acres for the town near Col. Hugh Montgomery's land.[2] This courthouse was a two story structure, approximately 40 by 50 feet, and had a courtroom on the first floor. This structure was later converted into a hotel and was not razed until the 1930s.[3]

A second courthouse was erected in 1855. This time the county put up a log and frame two story structure with wood siding. Larger than the first courthouse, it remained in use until it burned in 1885.[4]

The courthouse constructed in 1885 was a handsome two story brick structure featuring a tall center pavilion surmounted by a tall octagonal cupola. Two story wings housing county offices were located on the east and west sides. Stone was used to highlight window and door openings as well as for the foundation and belt course separating the first and second floors. This courthouse was destroyed by a fire in 1926.[5]

A vote was held in 1903 over relocating the county seat to LaFollette. While the vote to relocate was successful, the county court moved back to Jacksboro for the July 1904 court term.[6]

The present courthouse was completed in 1926. Because of concern over previous courthouse fires, this structure was constructed of brick, stone, steel and concrete. The architects were R.F. Graf & Sons and the contractors were Helms & Wills.[7] In 1964, a new wing was added to the courthouse.

An early view of the 1885 courthouse.

CANNON COUNTY

Formed: January 21, 1836
Formed from: Coffee, Warren, and Wilson Counties
County seat: Woodbury
Area: 266 sq.mi.

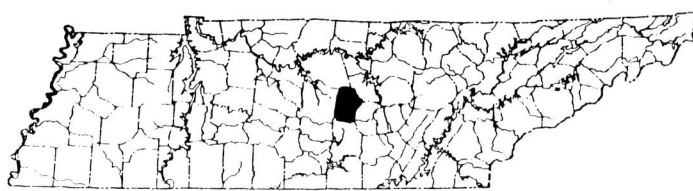

Cannon County was named for Newton Cannon, a veteran of the Creek War and the War of 1812. Cannon was also governor of Tennessee (1835-1839) and a U.S. Congressman (1814-17, 1821-27). The first court was held at the tavern of Henry D. McBroom in 1836.[1] This was a two story log or frame structure covered with clapboard siding.

Danville, the original name of the county seat, was changed to Woodbury (in honor of General Levi Woodbury, Secretary of the Treasury in President Andrew Jackson's Cabinet). The money raised from the sale of lots in the new county seat was used to build the first courthouse and jail.[2]

The second courthouse was built by William Bates for $13,000 in 1838 and was constructed on a three acre plot in the center of town. It was a two story brick structure on a stone foundation, quite plain in design. This courthouse had a square plan with a door on each side, with its front entrance facing south on Main Street. The windows on the first floor had arched heads, while those on the second were flat. The building was topped by a hip roof in the center of which was a cupola. This courthouse burned November 13, 1934.

Replaced in 1936 by the present courthouse, this structure was completed for $45,000. It is a handsome Neo-classical brick design on a stone foundation. It features two story stone classical pilasters and corner quoins on the slightly taller central section. In the center of the gable roof is a tall clock tower.

Left: Cannon County's first courthouse. Center: The second courthouse (1838). Right: The current courthouse under construction.

CARROLL COUNTY

Formed: March 11, 1821
Formed from: Western District
County seat: Huntingdon
Area: 599 sq.mi.

Carroll County was named for William Carroll, Governor of Tennessee from 1821-1827. The first court of Pleas and Quarter Sessions was held at the home of R.E.C. Dougherty.[1] The name of the county seat was originally Huntsville, being changed to Huntingdon in 1823.

The first courthouse was a small log cabin without a floor. Apparently built without a door *...Nathan Nesbit, chairman of the court of pleas and quarter sessions, blazed his way through the forest from his residence...carrying with him his cross-cut saw, with which he sawed the door out of the new court house and entered therein and opened the first court held at Huntingdon, December 9, 1822.*[2]

In 1824 the log courthouse was replaced by a frame structure 20 x 24 feet. This was used until around 1830, when a third, brick courthouse 30 x 50 feet was constructed. John Parker and Jacob Bledsoe built the foundations, George and John Simons were the brick masons, and Joel R. Smith was the carpenter. The second courthouse was sold to Robert Murray, who moved it to his lot on the east side of the square for use as a warehouse.[3]

A fourth, brick courthouse was constructed by Joel R. Smith and Thomas Banks for $12,000 around 1844. A two story brick structure on a stone foundation, this courthouse had an arched entry flanked by brick pilasters. This was topped by a pediment over the second floor. In the center of the hipped roof was an octagonal cupola. Enlarged in 1897, this courthouse burned in 1931.

The county's fifth, current courthouse was completed in 1931 at a cost of $100,000. Its design, by Hart, Freeland and Roberts Architects of Nashville, was influenced by the Lincoln Memorial in Washington, DC. A Neo-classical design, it features a pedimented portico on the front and engaged pedimented porticos on the sides.

Left: Carroll County's fourth courthouse. Right: The current courthouse c1930.

CARTER COUNTY

Formed: April 1796
Formed from: Washington County
County seat: Elizabethton
Area: 341 sq.mi.

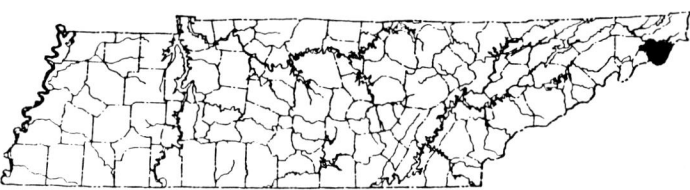

Carter County was the first county formed by the General Assembly of Tennessee, during the period between the adoption of the state constitution in February and formal admission the Union on June 1, 1796. It was named in honor of Landon Carter, the speaker of Senate of the State of Franklin and later its Secretary of State. The first court of Pleas and Quarter Sessions was probably organized in July 1796 at the home of Samuel Tipton. The third term was held in Elizabethton at the home of William Matlock in April 1797. Soon afterwards, court records indicate meetings being held at the courthouse.[1]

The county seat was established at Elizabethton (named for Elizabeth Carter, Landon Carter's wife). The first courthouse was a log structure probably constructed on the public square. It was used until 1820, when it was replaced by an octagonal structure, two stories in height. This second courthouse had a courtroom on the first floor and offices on the second. It was located in the center of the public square and was used until the completion of the present courthouse.[2]

In 1852 Carter County's third courthouse was built to plans drawn by Joseph S. Burts. The design called for a three story building with the county offices and court occupying the first and second floors. The third floor was used by the Masonic order. Built at a cost of $7,100, the contract went to John Lyle and William Fleming.[3]

Typical of several East Tennessee county courthouses, it featured a recessed portico with a pedimented gable. It also had stepped end gables typical of the residential architecture of the region. The center of the gable roof was topped by a domed octagonal cupola.

This courthouse was considerably rebuilt after a fire in 1933. At that time a number of design changes were made, including the addition of a projecting portico set on a one story base with stairways leading up from each side. The roof gable roof was changed to a hip and the cupola was not reconstructed.

Left: A c1880 view of the original design of the courthouse.
Right: A c1940 view of the rebuilt courthouse.

CHEATHAM COUNTY

Formed: February 28, 1856
Formed from: Davidson, Dickson, Montgomery, and Robertson Counties
County seat: Ashland City
Area: 303 sq.mi.

Cheatham County was named for Edward S. Cheatham, Speaker of the Senate when Cheatham County was created. The early county seats included Sycamore Powder Mills until 1856 and then Forest Hill until 1858. They were succeeded by Ashland, incorporated as Ashland City in 1859. The first court was held in May of 1856.

The first courthouse (1856) was a log building at Sycamore Powder Mills. It was used for two court sessions. The court then moved to Leeland Meeting House at Forest Hill, where its sessions were held until 1858.

The second courthouse was a two story frame building at the corner of Main and Cumberland, built for $2,000. It was used until 1869, at which time it was sold and was converted into the Central Hotel.[1]

A more substantial brick courthouse was constructed for $12,000 in 1869. This building was two storys, 42 x 48 feet, with the county offices on the first floor and the courtroom on the second. In 1914 a new two story brick wing, 42 x 48 feet, was constructed on the front of the courthouse at a cost of $25,000. This was designed by architect R.E. Tubeville.[2]

A large jail addition to the rear of the courthouse was completed in 1986.

CHESTER COUNTY

Formed: March 1, 1879
Formed from: Hardeman, Henderson, Madison, and McNairy Counties
County seat: Henderson
Area: 289 sq.mi.

Chester County was initially designated as Wisdom County by the state legislature in 1875. It was re-erected out of the same fractions in 1879 and renamed for Colonel Robert I. Chester, a veteran of the War of 1812 and United States Marshall of the Western District.[1] The county seat, Henderson, was selected by vote over Montezuma, and was named in honor of Colonel James Henderson, also a veteran of the War of 1812.

The courts met in several locations until the purchase of the residence and grounds of the late Dr. J.A. Crook in 1883. The four acres and large two story frame house were purchased for $3,000 and the house was converted for use as offices and courtroom.[2] From the historic photograph, this building appears to have been remodelled (or rebuilt) in brick. It had paired arched windows and a tower over the entry porch. This structure was destroyed by fire in 1910.

The present courthouse, a two story brick Classical Revival style structure, was completed in 1913. Sitting on a tall base, the building features a two story pedimented four column portico. It has a low hip roof with an open square, domed cupola.

A view of Chester County's late 19th century courthouse.

CLAIBORNE COUNTY

Formed: October 29, 1801
Formed from: Grainger and Hawkins Counties
County seat: Tazewell
Area: 434 sq.mi.

Claiborne County was named in honor of William C.C. Claiborne, the Governor of the Mississippi Territory. Claiborne was a judge of the Superior Court of Tennessee, a congressman from Tennessee, and later the Governor of Louisiana. The first court of Pleas and Quarter Sessions was held at house of John Owens in December 1801. The next term was held at the home of John Hunt (on the site of Tazewell), while a third term was held at the home of Elisha Walling.[1]

It was not until 1804 that a small frame courthouse was erected at Tazewell.[2] Tazewell, the county seat, was named for the well-known Virginia Tazewell family and was probably laid out in 1802 or 1803.

The second courthouse, constructed c1850, burned in 1932. That courthouse followed a similar plan and design to others in East Tennessee. It was a two story brick structure with a recessed portico. Massive brick pillars supported the pedimented gable over the portico. On the main gable roof was a square cupola.

The current Claiborne County courthouse was completed in 1932. Bauman and Bauman, Architects designed the building in a Neo-classical style. It is a brick, three story structure trimmed in stone and includes a handsome pedimented two story stone portico set on a rusticated stone base. The first floor is separated from the upper floors by a stone belt course at the height of the portico's stone base. This courthouse was constructed by V.L. Nicholson Company of Knoxville for $150,000.

Claiborne County's second courthouse.

CLAY COUNTY

Formed: December 7, 1870
Formed from: Jackson and Overton Counties
County seat: Celina
Area: 236 sq.mi.

Clay County was named in honor of Henry Clay, congressman and senator from Kentucky. Clay was also Speaker of the House of Representatives and was Secretary of State under John Quincy Adams. The first session of the county court was held in a store belonging to Mary Roberts in Butler's Landing. The county seat, Celina (named for the daughter of pioneer educator Moses Fisk), was selected over Butler's Landing and Bennett's Ferry in a narrow vote.[1]

The courthouse was begun in 1872 and was completed for $9,999. D.L. Dow of Cookeville was the contractor. The completion date was set for October 1, 1873, and the first court session was held in the courthouse in June of 1874. The brick for the courthouse is said to have been made from the clay taken from the public square and all of the lumber used was hand-dressed.

A two story structure, it is very plain, but elegant in design. The second floor, which accommodates the courtroom, is considerably taller than the first floor. The elaborate arched window in the courtroom is directly over the arched main entrance to the courthouse. The structure has a simple bracketed cornice and a low hip roof, in the center of which is a square cupola with a tall pyramidal roof. The building has been in constant use since it opened.[2]

Left: Interior courthouse office view taken in 1923. Right: A postcard view of the courthouse c1950.

COCKE COUNTY

Formed: October 9, 1797
Formed from: Jefferson County
County seat: Newport
Area: 434 sq.mi.

Cocke County was named in honor of Senator William Cocke, an officer in the Revolutionary War and a leader of the State of Franklin. Cocke was also one of the first U.S. senators from Tennessee. The first courthouse, said to be a log structure, was built in Oldtown on the French Broad River. Oldtown continued as county seat until 1868, when it moved to Clinton (Newport).

The second courthouse at Oldtown was constructed of brick in 1828. This was a simple two story structure, nearly square in plan and had a low pitched gable roof. It was used until 1868 when the county seat was relocated to Clinton on the Pigeon River. The third courthouse, a rented structure at the corner of Broadway and Mims Avenue, burned in 1876. After the fire, the county seat moved back to Oldtown and into the 1828 courthouse.

With the completion of the railroad to Newport, agitation began for again moving the county seat. In 1884 the courts returned to Newport and occupied a fourth courthouse which was completed in 1886 for $10,000. This courthouse was erected on the site of the current courthouse. It was a two story brick structure with a tall mansard roofed tower. The building had a low pitched hip roof and an elaborate cornice at the eave. Hooded arched windows were used on the second floor. A fire on May 29, 1930 totlly destroyed the Trustee's office.[1]

The present courthouse, completed in 1931, was constructed at a cost of $110,000. Designed by Manley and Young, Architects of Knoxville in the Classical Revival style, it is a three story brick structure with heavy stone quoins at the corners. Projecting end pavilions flank the center section with its five tall arched courtroom windows on the second floor. In 1979 the courtroom was remodelled.[2]

Left: An early log structure which may have been the first courthouse.[3] Right: The 1884 courthouse.

COFFEE COUNTY

Formed: January 8, 1836
Formed from: Bedford, Franklin, and Warren Counties
County seat: Manchester
Area: 429 sq.mi.

Coffee County was named in honor of Major General John Coffee, who fought in the New Orleans campaign of 1814. The first sessions of county court were held in a log house used by Baptists as church. This continued until 1837, when a two-story brick courthouse was erected.[1] This structure cost $10,000 and burned in December 1870.

The present courthouse built was in 1871 at a cost of $23,071 and is a two story brick structure. The courtroom and quarters of the county officers were on the first floor, while the second floor housed the circuit court and jury rooms.[2]

Until 1914 the courthouse had four rooms downstairs with two cross halls. On the second floor was the courtroom, two jury rooms, and hallway. Alterations in 1914-15 resulted in an addition on the north side for a trustee's office, restrooms, and a stairway. The east-west halls were closed and made into vaults between the four corner rooms. The courtroom was also enlarged to seat up to 300.

There has been much debate over the fate of this historic courthouse as there has never been adequate space in the present building. Voters rejected a bond issue for a new building in 1968 and the courthouse underwent a complete remodeling in 1968-74. This included a new roof and exterior repairs (including cupola and metal ornaments).[3]

Another battle over demolition in 1977 saw the voters again rejecting a bond issue to replace the building.

Left: c1960 view of the Coffee County Courthouse. Right: 1896 view of the courthouse during a parade by the ladies of the millinery department of Winston's, celebrating its opening.

CROCKETT COUNTY

Formed: November 23, 1871
Formed from: Dyer, Gibson, Madison, and Haywood Counties
County seat: Alamo
Area: 265 sq.mi.

Originally established in 1845 as an "Act to establish Crockett County in honor of and to perpetuate the memory of David Crockett, one of Tennessee's distinguished sons." In 1846 it was decided that this was not a constitutional county. Crockett became a county again in 1871 after overcoming considerable opposition from the old counties from which it was formed.

The county seat, originally called Cageville, was changed to Alamo after the Alamo in Texas where David Crockett lost his life. The initial court sessions were held in the Odd Fellows and Masonic halls until sometime in 1873, when the records were removed to a large wood frame carriage factory building (later the Fouchee Hotel), where they were held until the courthouse was completed in 1875.

Crockett County's first courthouse continues on in use today. It was built from designs by architect John Archer of Brownsville. Goodspeed provides an early description of this building, saying that the courthouse was a ...*large, two-story brick, with four entrances and cross halls. On the first floor are the offices of the county court clerk, sheriff, register and two additional offices. On the second floor are the offices of the circuit court clerk and the clerk and master of the chancery court, and also the circuit court room, which is a large, ventilated and commodious room. The building is surmounted with an observatory, guarded by iron railings, the same having been constructed with a view of placing them in a clock tower. The court house cost about $25,000, and is claimed to be the finest of its kind in West Tennessee.*[1]

As completed in brick, the building was 55 x 96 feet and was two stories high. Entrances were located on all four elevations. In the center of the hipped roof was a square clock tower with a mansard roof. The building was constructed by E.R. Crandall of Brownsville for $20,495.[2]

During a 1934 remodeling the courthouse was substantially altered. The hipped roof and clock tower were removed at that time. In addition, the building was given a stucco finish scored to look like stone. Later alterations included the replacement of the original windows with modern windows which were designed to accommodate the lowered interior ceilings.

Left: The courthouse as originally completed. Right: The courthouse c1960.

CUMBERLAND COUNTY

Formed: November 16, 1855
Formed from: Bledsoe, Morgan, Putnam, Rhea, Roane, White, and Van Buren Counties
County seat: Crossville
Area: 682 sq.mi.

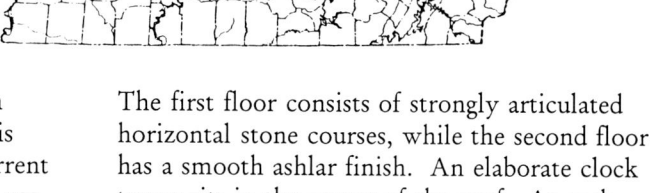

Named for the Cumberland Mountains, **Cumberland County's** first courthouse was a log structure completed in 1857. It was used until 1886, when it was sold for $25.00.[1] A second, permanent second courthouse was built of local sandstone in 1886 at a cost of $2,500. It was a two story structure with a low hip roof. Quite simple in design, an important feature was the square cupola with its tall pyramidal roof over its front entrance. An iron picket fence set the courthouse apart from the street. This courthouse was dam aged by fire in 1905.[2] At that time, a decision was made to construct a new courthouse. This earlier structure, across the street from the current courthouse, was renovated and is currently in use by the local geneaological society.

The current courthouse was constructed of Indiana limestone at a cost of $23,000 and was completed in 1905. A two story structure, it features a monumental entrance consisting of paired arches over which are large windows and a stepped gable. The first floor consists of strongly articulated horizontal stone courses, while the second floor has a smooth ashlar finish. An elaborate clock tower sits in the center of the roof. At each corner are found unusual, slightly lower projecting octagonal bays.

Right: An early postcard view of the current courthouse.
Left: Cumberland County's second courthouse.

DAVIDSON COUNTY

Formed: October 6, 1783
Formed from: Washington County
County seat: Nashville
Area: 502 sq.mi.

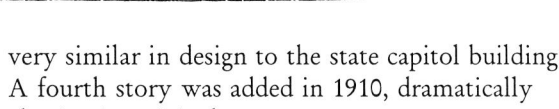

Davidson County was formed by an act of the North Carolina legislature and originally included most of the territory west of the Cumberland Mountains now included in Middle Tennessee.[1] The county was named in honor of Brigadier General William Lee Davidson of North Carolina, who was killed in the Revolutionary War.

The first courthouse, built in 1784, was constructed of hewn logs and was 18 feet square with a lean-to addition of 12 feet. Prior to building a second, more permanent courthouse in 1802, a Methodist church was used. Of the second, or "lost" courthouse, no description is known.

The third courthouse was completed in 1830. It was a three story Federal style structure with a low hipped roof on which was a cupola and bell tower. This building burned in 1856.

Francis Strickland, son of William Strickland, designed the fourth courthouse. Completed in 1857 in the Greek Revival style, this building was

very similar in design to the state capitol building. A fourth story was added in 1910, dramatically altering its original appearance.

The present courthouse was completed in 1937 at a cost of $2,000,000. The architects were Emmons H. Woolwine of Nashville and Fredrick C. Hirons of New York. Designed in the Art Deco style, this structure features handsome interior murals executed by Dean Cornwell.

Left: The third courthouse. Top Center: The fourth courthouse. Bottom Center: The fourth courthouse with its added third floor. Right: A postcard view of the current courthouse still partially surrounded by the original courthouse square buildings.

DECATUR COUNTY

Formed: November, 1845
Formed from: Perry County
County seat: Decaturville
Area: 333 sq.mi.

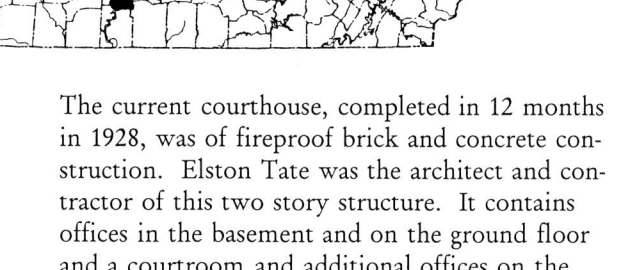

Decatur County was named in honor of Commodore Stephen Decatur. The drive for a new county was led by Samuel Brasher and included 200 voters. They banded together to push to form a new county on the west side of the Tennessee River which at that time divided Perry County.[1] Decaturville, the current name of the county seat, was originally Decaturboro. This name-ending change took place in several Tennessee towns after the War of 1812 between the United States and Great Britain.[2]

The first court met in 1848 in a log cabin on the west side of the public square. Shortly after (c1849), a two story frame courthouse was erected.

This was destroyed by fire on July 3, 1869, together with most of the records.

A third courthouse was completed for $9,000 in 1869.[3] This was a two story brick structure that had the county offices on the first floor and the courtroom on the second. This courthouse also burned, again with most of its records, on May 27, 1927. The county offices were then moved to the Eli Vise store, a two story building on the southeast corner of the public square. The courts met in the Decaturville School building.[4]

The current courthouse, completed in 12 months in 1928, was of fireproof brick and concrete construction. Elston Tate was the architect and contractor of this two story structure. It contains offices in the basement and on the ground floor and a courtroom and additional offices on the second floor. The building underwent a complete $200,000 facelift and renovation in 1975, which included the creation of additional office spaces in basement.[5]

Two views of the third, 1869 courthouse. The view on the right shows the decorative brick pattern on the main elevation.

DEKALB COUNTY

Formed: December 11, 1837
Formed from: Cannon, Warren, and White Counties
County seat: Smithville
Area: 304 sq.mi.

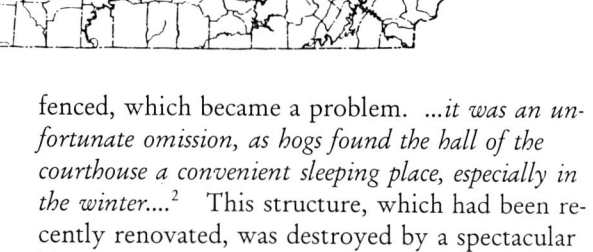

DeKalb County was named in honor of Baron Johann DeKalb, a friend of American liberty, who fell at the Battle of Camden in the Revolutionary War. The first courts were held at the home of Bernard Richardson, at Fall Creek. Richardson also donated the 50 acres for the county seat. Smithville was named for Samuel Granville Smith, first mayor of Gainesboro and the Tennessee Secretary of State at the time of his death in 1835.[1]

A log courthouse was soon erected and functioned until 1840. A second, permanent courthouse was the constructed. This building was located to the north of the center of the public square and was a square, two story brick structure with a gable roof that cost $6,000. The first floor contained four offices while the courtroom was located on the second floor. An octagonal cupola with a domed roof was located towards one end of the roof. A fence was soon added around the courthouse to keep out roaming livestock.

A third courthouse was completed in the center of the public square in 1890. This courthouse was also a two story brick structure with a metal shingle hipped roof. A square cupola with a pyramidal roof was located in the center of the main roof. The area around this courthouse was not fenced, which became a problem. ...*it was an unfortunate omission, as hogs found the hall of the courthouse a convenient sleeping place, especially in the winter....*[2] This structure, which had been recently renovated, was destroyed by a spectacular blaze in 1925, begun by a fire in the almost-new General Stores building on south side of the square. Sparks from this fire, it appears, ignited bird nests in courthouse cupola.

The fourth courthouse, completed in 1925, was a fireproof concrete, steel, and brick structure. It was torn down in 1970 and replaced by the present steel and granite Model Cities project courthouse. The fifth courthouse cost $750,000 and was designed by Maffett-Howland and Associates.

Left: The second courthouse, 1872, the Presswood hanging. Center: The third, 1890 courthouse. Right: The fourth, 1925 courthouse.

DICKSON COUNTY

Formed: October 3, 1803
Formed from: Montgomery and Robertson Counties
County seat: Charlotte
Area: 490 sq.mi.

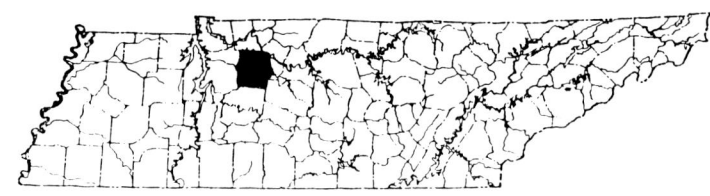

Dickson County was named in honor of William Dickson, physician and member of Congress representing the Mero District. The first county and circuit courts were held at the home of James Nesbit, at Barton's Creek near Charlotte (named for Charlotte Robertson, the wife of James Robertson and one of the early settlers in Middle Tennessee). When Charlotte became the county seat in 1806, a central lot was reserved for the courthouse. The county's buildings, financed by the sale of town lots, appear to have been completed between 1810 and 1812.

The courthouse was to be 24 x 32 feet, partitioned into four or more offices. The county officials were not sure whether to use brick or wood in the new structure, but that the work was to be done "...in an elegant manner." The work began immediately, and the result was a large two story brick courthouse with a large, octagonal belfry on the hip roof, that cost between $10,000-12,000.[1]

The actual completion date of the original courthouse remains uncertain as the records of this period were destroyed in 1830 when a tornado hit this courthouse (and the courthouse in Shelbyville, Bedford County).[2] The courthouse was rebuilt in the same place, style, and manner, for about the same cost in 1831 by architect-builder Phillip Murray of Charlotte.[3] Two story brick wings were added to either side of the courthouse in 1930. While the style was retained, it was impossible to match the original brick and the entire structure was covered with the new brick used for the construction of the wings.

From 1819-1821 the Tennessee Supreme Court held its sessions here. This courthouse is the oldest courthouse in continuous use in the state.

A view of the 1831 courthouse in the late 19th century.

DYER COUNTY

Formed: October 16, 1823
Formed from: Western District
County seat: Dyersburg
Area: 510 sq.mi.

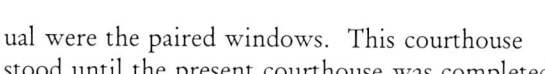

Dyer County was named in honor of Colonel Henry Dyer, who served under Andrew Jackson in the Natchez Expedition, the Creek War of 1812 and the Seminole War of 1818. In October of 1824 the Court of Pleas and Quarter Sessions was convened at the house of John Warren, where it continued until 1826, when the county seat was established at Dyersburg. Joel H. Dyer gave the initial 60 acres for the new county seat.[1]

The first courthouse is thought to have been built of logs by Elias Dement.[2] It stood at the northwest corner of the present courthouse yard. In 1827 a two story log courthouse was built on the public square. This was replaced in 1836 by a one story wood frame courthouse.[3]

Dyer County's third courthouse was a two story brick structure built in 1850. This building was burned, along with the county records, by the Union Army in 1864.[4] Following the Civil War, a fourth courthouse, incorporating the walls of the fourth building, was completed in 1867 at a cost of $8,000. Square in plan, it had a simple Greek Revival design featuring two story pilasters and a full entablature below the hip roof. Unusual were the paired windows. This courthouse stood until the present courthouse was completed.

The current courthouse, Dyer County's fifth, was completed in 1912. It is again a two story brick structure with two story pilasters and a full entablature. A low parapet wall conceals the low pitch roof on which a round domed cupola sits.

Left: The log residence used for the first Dyer County Courts. Center: The fourth courthouse. Right: The current Dyer County Courthouse c1955.

FAYETTE COUNTY

Formed: September 29, 1824
Formed from: Shelby and Hardeman Counties
County seat: Somerville
Area: 705 sq.mi.

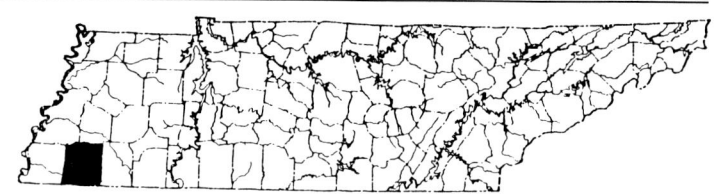

Fayette County was named for the Marquis de Lafayette. The first court of Pleas and Quarter Sessions was held at the home of Robert G. Thornton from December 1824 to November 1825. In December of 1825 Somerville was established as the county seat. Somerville was named for Robert Somerville, who was killed leading a charge against the Creek indians in 1814 at the Battle of Horseshoe Bend.

The first court session was held in November of 1825 in a temporary log cabin on the public square. This structure was approximately 20 feet square and court records show that it had one window and two doors. This building was also used as a church as well as for other public meetings.

The second courthouse was a brick structure with a cupola on top and was built in 1833 by Joseph Coe. It was 50 x 60 feet and was located in the center of the town square, which was fenced. It apparently presented many repair problems, was heated with wood burning stoves, and had carpet on the floor.

A third courthouse was completed in 1876 at a cost of $45,000. Designed by Jones and Baldwin of Memphis[1], it was constructed of brick and had a large tower in the front and two smaller towers to the rear. A statue of Justice with sword and balance stood on top of the main tower. The slate roof was trimmed with galvanized iron painted a stone color. This structure burned on February 10, 1925.[2]

Details of the third courthouse included tall entry doors of carved walnut, an entry lobby with grand stairways leading to the second floor, and a courtroom with tall windows on three sides and chandeliers hanging from its vaulted ceilings.[3] At the time of its construction it was considered one of the most beautiful and best planned courthouses in West Tennessee.

The current courthouse was designed by architect George Mahan, Jr. Plans for the building were finished within 6 weeks of fire and it was completed in 1926 at a cost of $106,000.[4] Built of buff colored brick, it features a domed copper roof and a clock tower over its Ionic-columned entry portico. On the interior, the courthouse has a central rotunda with a marble wainscot and marble steps. The courthouse was renovated in 1984-85 at cost of $250,000 by Grace and Associates of Bartlett.[5]

The third courthouse with its tall main tower. The tower roof was topped with an elaborate cupola. One of the smaller rear towers can be partially seen at the far left.

FENTRESS COUNTY

Formed: November 28, 1823
Formed from: Morgan and Overton Counties
County seat: Jamestown
Area: 499 sq.mi.

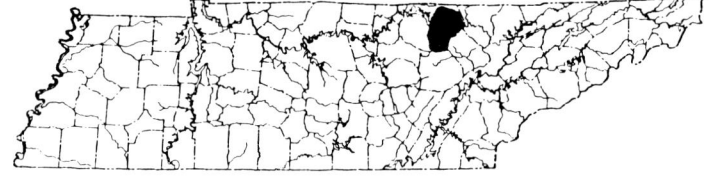

Fentress County was named for James Fentress, a prominent Tennessee legislator and later an officer in Confederate Army. The first court was held at Three Forks on the Wolf's River.[1] The first courthouse was built in 1828, when there were only five families in town. Plans for the courthouse were developed by John M. Clemons, the father of Mark Twain, who was the first circuit court clerk for the county.[2]

The first courthouse, for which an extensive written description survives, was destroyed by fire in the 1860s. It indicates that this was to be a one story structure, 40 x 27 feet. The structure was to be divided into a nearly square courtroom and two jury rooms at one end. Apparently the details presented provided an option for either a brick or a hewn log structure. No indication was given as to which material was actually used in its construction. Also, if no details were given by the commissioners, the plan was to follow that of the courthouse at Gainesborough (Gainesboro, Jackson County).[3]

The second courthouse, a two story brick structure on a stone base and having a low hip roof, was completed in 1865. It was a simple structure, three bays wide with large 9-over-9 double-hung shuttered windows. This courthouse was also destroyed by fire, on December 8, 1904.

In April 1905, the county issued $15,000 in bonds for a third courthouse. W. Chamberlin & Co. of Knoxville was hired to prepare the design.[4] Construction problems resulted in the architect and contractor being discharged in November of 1906. Finally completed and occupied in 1908, it is a two story stone structure with slightly lower two story stone north and south wings. The central hip roof is surmounted by a square clock tower. In 1973 the north and south wings were extended.

Left: The second courthouse. Center: The third courthouse under construction. Right: The third as originally completed.

FRANKLIN COUNTY

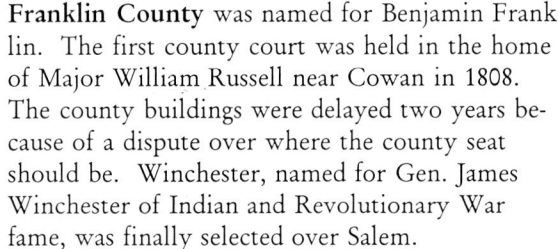

Formed: December 3, 1807
Formed from: Bedford and Warren Counties
County seat: Winchester
Area: 553 sq.mi.

Franklin County was named for Benjamin Franklin. The first county court was held in the home of Major William Russell near Cowan in 1808. The county buildings were delayed two years because of a dispute over where the county seat should be. Winchester, named for Gen. James Winchester of Indian and Revolutionary War fame, was finally selected over Salem.

The first courthouse was constructed where the current courthouse now stands. It was a small brick structure completed in 1814. This structure is believed to have been a two story, 40 x 40 foot square building that served its purposes for nearly 25 years. It was torn down in 1839 and the local Presbyterians allowed their church to be used while the new courthouse was being completed.

The second courthouse was not completed until 1842. James Robinson was paid $80 for plans and specifications for this structure. William Reeves and Adam Oehmig were the contractors, and the final cost was around $10,000. In this two story brick structure, the county offices were located on the second floor, while the courtroom was on the first floor, the opposite of most courthouse planning of the period. In 1890, the courthouse was modernized with Victorian embellishments including decorative work on the eaves and an a redesigned tower.[1] It functioned until 1937, when the third and current courthouse was completed.

Cramped offices, the pressure for additional space, the inability to expand into the attic and signs of structural fatigue pushed the replacement of the second courthouse. Planning for the current Art Deco style courthouse began in 1935. It was designed by Marr and Holman Architects of Nashville and constructed by Niles E. Yearwood of Nashville for $142,000. In their design for the courthouse, Marr and Holman raised the formerly level site in order to provide a convenient basement floor with ample windows. The symmetrical plan features the traditional clock tower. Here, in an effort to cut down its weight and simplify the support structure, this central tower was finished with sheet-metal.[2] In 1992 an elevator tower became the first major exterior alteration to this structure.

The second courthouse with its 1890 Victorian embellishments.

GIBSON COUNTY

Formed: October 21, 1823
Formed from: Western District
County seat: Trenton
Area: 603 sq.mi.

Gibson County was named after Colonel John H. Gibson. The earliest courts were held at the home of Luke Biggs, four miles from Trenton. In 1826 a temporary courthouse was constructed at the county seat of Gibsonport (the name was changed to Trenton in 1826). This structure was one story, roughly 20 x 35 feet in size, and constructed of hewn logs. It had a rough plank floor and a clapboard roof. A log partition at one end formed a jury room 10 x 20 feet in size.[1]

The log courthouse was replaced by a two story brick structure in 1829. Costing $5,988[2], this building stood until 1837, when it was determined to be unsafe and was demolished and replaced by a temporary building erected of the same materials at a cost of $399. This structure was one story high, 36 x 22 feet, with a 12 foot interior ceiling height, and had two doors and four windows.[3] Solomon Shaw and Robert Jetton of Trenton were the contractor-builders.[4]

A two story brick courthouse, 42 x 66 feet was completed in 1841. This structure had a hipped roof with a gable over the main entrance and was topped by an octagonal domed cupola. The contractors were Solomon Shaw and Robert Jetton. Built for $20,000, it served until 1899, when it was demolished for the current courthouse as it had become inadequate for conducting the county's business.

The county's fifth courthouse was begun in 1899 and was completed in 1901. This structure was designed by Walter Chamberlain & Co. of Knoxville.[5] The contract award to Hugger and Winston of Atlanta for $32,500 was re-awarded to T.R. Biggs & Sons in 1900 because of significant construction delays. They required an additional $14,000 to complete the building.[6] The courthouse was described at the time as being ...*in all respects a modern structure, designed and constructed with an intelligent and comprehensive regard for the wants of a great and growing county.*[7] The clock tower, destroyed by fire in 1941, been rebuilt with modifications to the original design.

Left: Gibson County's fourth courthouse. Right: The current courthouse prior to 1941.

GILES COUNTY

Formed: November 14, 1809
Formed from: Maury
County seat: Pulaski
Area: 611 sq.mi.

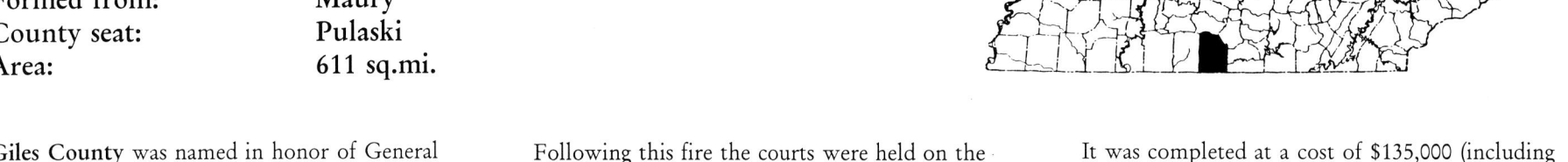

Giles County was named in honor of General William B. Giles, Governor of Virginia and U.S. Senator supporting Tennessee's admission to the Union. The first court met at the home of Lewis Kirk at Richland Creek where a rough log structure had been erected in his yard for the court sessions.[1]

With the establishment of Pulaski (named for the Revolutionary War hero, Polish Count Casmir Pulaski) as the county seat in 1811, lots were sold and cane was cut on the public square where a courthouse was constructed. This structure, built of round logs covered with clapboards, stood about where the south gate of the present courthouse now stands.[2] It burned two years later *...presumably by the citizens, they having become impatient and indignant at the delay of the commissioners in giving them a more commodious and sightly building.*[3]

The county then contracted with Archibald Alexander of Pulaski for a new courthouse. Completed in 1815, this was a substantial two story brick structure. It was, however, torn down about 1850 and replaced with a larger and finer brick courthouse. It caught fire in its cornice from a defective flue and was destroyed in 1856.

Following this fire the courts were held on the first floor of the Odd Fellows Hall until the next courthouse was completed in 1859. Architect Adolphus Heiman of Nashville furnished the plan and directed its erection.[4] Completed at a cost of $27,000, this courthouse was one of the state's finest. Again a two story brick building, it was designed in the Greek Revival style and included arched two story porticoes on each elevation and engaged pilasters on the exterior walls. The building was topped by a low hipped roof and a tall domed octagonal cupola. It burned in 1907.

The current courthouse, completed in 1909, was designed by Benjamin N. Smith of Montgomery.

It was completed at a cost of $135,000 (including furnishings) by contractor George Moore & Sons of Nashville. A large, two story brick structure, it is 60 x 150 feet and has a large central cupola.

Left: The current courthouse in 1925. Right: View of the 1859 courthouse during the hanging of Sam Davis.

GRAINGER COUNTY

Formed: 1796
Formed from: Hawkins and Knox Counties
County seat: Rutledge
Area: 280 sq.mi.

One of the initial counties created by the Tennessee state legislature, **Grainger County** was named for Mary Grainger, the wife of Governor William Blount. It is the only county in the state named for a woman. The location of the county seat proved to be difficult, and it was not settled until 1801.[1] Until that time the courts met at various places. Rutledge, the county seat, was named for General George Rutledge, a prominent pioneer.[2]

Grainger's first courthouse was erected in 1801 by Francis Mayberry.[3] This was, apparently, a small frame structure. It was occupied until it was replaced in 1848 by a small brick courthouse. This building was later purchased by members of the Presbyterian church.

The third courthouse was completed in 1848.[4] It was of typical regional design, a two story brick structure incorporating a recessed pedimented portico. A square cupola was located in the center of the gable roof. This was followed by a fourth courthouse in 1904.

Built by M.T. Lewman & Co. of Louisville, this was a two story brick building with a stone arched principal entrance, above the second floor of which was a stepped gable. Behind this rose a tall square clock tower. Projecting two story pavilions with pyramidal roofs were found at each corner of this courthouse. This courthouse burned in 1946.

The current courthouse, Grainger's fifth, was completed in 1949 at a cost of $300,000. It was designed by architects W.W. Griffin and S.G. Goodwyne in the simple Art Moderne post-war style.[5]

Top: Grainger County's second courthouse (1848). Bottom: The fourth courthouse (1904).

GREENE COUNTY

Formed: 1783
Formed from: Washington County
County seat: Greeneville
Area: 622 sq.mi.

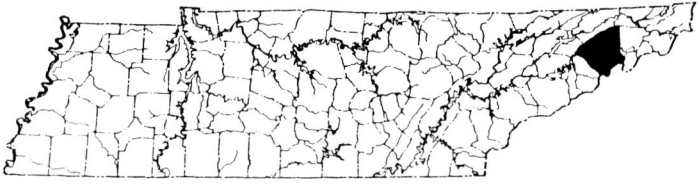

Greene County was created by the state of North Carolina and named in honor of General Nathaniel Green, a Major General of the Revolutionary War. The court of Pleas and Quarter Sessions first met at the house of Robert Carr near Big Spring in Greeneville.

The first courthouse, built around 1785, was constructed of logs and was used until 1804-05. Here, the third Franklin convention was held in November 1785. The courthouse was described by the historian Ramsey as: *...built of unhewn logs and covered with clapboards and was occupied by the court at first without a floor or loft. It had one opening only for an entrance, which was not yet provided with a shutter. Windows were not needed, either for ventilation or light, the intervals between the logs being a good substitute for them.*[1]

This structure was replaced around 1805 by another structure, of which nothing is known. The next courthouse was a two story brick structure constructed in 1822-23. Designed in the Greek Revival style, the facades were divided into bays by two story brick pilasters. The front elevation featured a recessed entry porch over which was a pedimented gable and an octagonal domed cupola. An addition containing four offices and two staircases was added in 1870.

The current, fourth courthouse was constructed for $40,000 in 1916 in the neo-Classical style. It was designed by the architect Thomas S. Brown.[2] This two story structure, built of brick and stone, features front and side Ionic porticoes. The porticoes are finished in stone, as are the corner quoins and main entablature.

Left: The current courthouse under construction. Right: The third, Neo-classical style courthouse.

GRUNDY COUNTY

Formed: January 29, 1844
Formed from: Coffee and Warren Counties
County seat: Altamont
Area: 361 sq.mi.

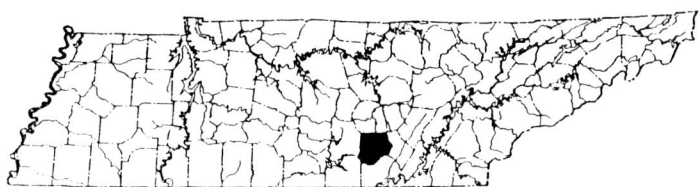

Grundy County was named in honor of Felix Grundy, a U.S. senator and congressman as well as attorney-general in the cabinet of President Martin Van Buren. Prior to 1848 the court was held at the home of Jesse Wooten in Beersheba Springs[1] (also known as Wooten Cabins). Altamont became the county seat in 1848. The first courthouse built there burned in 1853. For a period of time Tracy City became the county seat.

A second courthouse was constructed at Altamont in 1885. It was a simple two story brick structure, Victorian in style. This building had a simple mansard roof and a corner tower. In 1958 an annex was constructed, also two stories and of brick construction. This courthouse was burned in an arson fire on May 3, 1990 with a complete loss of tax, court and election records.

After the fire, county offices were scattered in various buildings. However, by November of 1990, all of the county offices were reunited in the Altamont City Hall.

Grundy County's new courthouse was occupied in April of 1996. Designed by the Architectural Office of Williams, Inc. of Franklin, TN, it is a two story brick structure in the Neo-classical style. It features a projecting pedimented portico main entrance. The building has a low hip roof with an octagonal cupola in the center.

Left: Early view of the 1885 courthouse. Right: The courthouse following the May 1990 fire.

HAMBLEN COUNTY

Formed: May 31, 1870
Formed from: Grainger, Hawkins, and Jefferson Counties
County seat: Morristown
Area: 161 sq.mi.

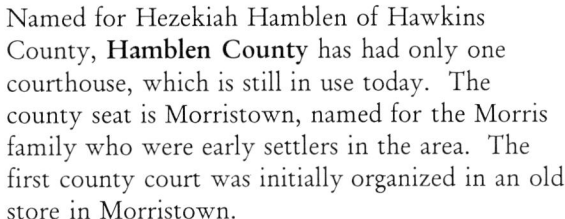

Named for Hezekiah Hamblen of Hawkins County, **Hamblen County** has had only one courthouse, which is still in use today. The county seat is Morristown, named for the Morris family who were early settlers in the area. The first county court was initially organized in an old store in Morristown.

Hamblen County's courthouse was designed by Knoxville architect A.C. Bruce and was completed in 1874. Bruce drew up and presented three plans, costing $10,000, $15,000, and $18,000. Adopted was the $18,000 plan, with the award going to contractors George W. Folsom and John Lyle. The final construction cost was $21,750. In Bruce's design, the courthouse was to face south, include a balcony for speakers at rallies, and place the courtroom on the second floor.[1]

Basically a three story structure, because of the sloping site, it has only a two story appearance from one side. The final design for the building included a tall central pavilion and slightly lower flanking wings, all of which are embellished with quoins at the corners. On the three story front pavilion is found Bruce's two story balcony. The roof is a combination of low hip and gable construction, mansard roof components and a tall, mansard-roofed cupola in the center. In the early 1950s, wings matching the original design were added to each side of the courthouse to provide space for record vaults and offices.

Design changes in 1968 were completed by Morristown architects Community Tectonics, Inc. These changes resulted in additional floor and vault space as well as the walls of the courthouse being painted grey and were completed at a cost of $300,000.

Views of the principal elevations of the Hamblen County Courthouse prior to the construction of the wings.

HAMILTON COUNTY

Formed: October 25, 1819
Formed from: Rhea County
County seat: Chattanooga
Area: 543 sq.mi.

Hamilton County was named in honor of Alexander Hamilton, a leader of the American Revolution and secretary of the Treasury under President Washington. The first courts were held at Poe's Tavern at Poe's Crossroads. Asahel Rawling's farm was used next. Here, a log courthouse was constructed. A village grew up around this called Hamilton County Courthouse (also called Dallas). This remained the county seat until 1840, when an election moved this to Harrison (named for General William Henry Harrison), where a substantial brick courthouse was built by Thomas Crutchfield.[1]

Following a vote in 1870 to move the county seat to Chattanooga, the county court used existing buildings until 1879, when a courthouse site was selected. During the 1870-79 period the courts and county offices occupied James Hall on the northeast corner of Market and Sixth. They later bought property at the southwest corner of Market and Fourth, fitting this building out as a courthouse and jail. This pre-Civil War structure continued in use as the courthouse until 1879.

The next courthouse was designed by architect A.C. Bruce of Chattanooga and Patten & McIntuff were the contractors. It cost $100,325 and was completed in 1879. For this courthouse a new location, the J.L. Atkins lot, was selected.

The new courthouse was sited in the center of this new square. Bruce's design was a two story brick structure with stone trim and featured mansard roofed towers, including a dominant tall corner clock tower. In 1891 the courthouse was remodelled and greatly enlarged at a cost of $50,000 to designs by architect William H. Floyd. Included were ceiling frescoes on the circuit courtroom ceiling. This courthouse continued in use until it was destroyed by fire in 1910. Following the fire, the courts were moved to the municipal building.[2]

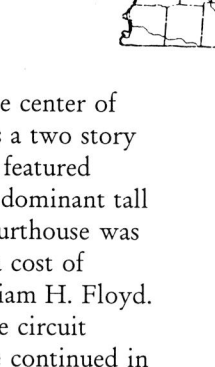

The current courthouse was completed in 1913 at a cost of $350,000 to Neo-classical designs by Chattanooga architect Reuben H. Hunt and built by George A. Fuller, contractor. Located on the site of the previous courthouse, this structure was constructed of Tennessee grey marble. Unusual features are its glazed tile roof and colored glass dome.[3]

Left: Poe's Tavern, site of the first Hamilton County courts. Right: The 1879 courthouse designed by A.C. Bruce with alterations by W.H. Floyd.

HANCOCK COUNTY

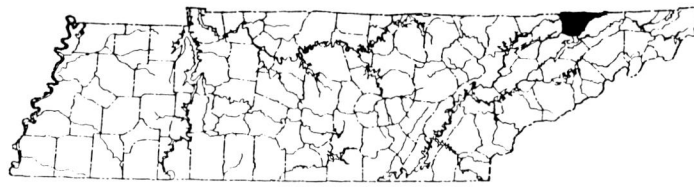

Formed:	January 7, 1844
Formed from:	Claiborne and Hawkins Counties
County seat:	Sneedville
Area:	222 sq.mi.

Hancock County, formed in 1844, was not organized until 1846 because of constitutional objections. The county was named for John Hancock, a Revolutionary War leader, president of the Continental Congress and first signer of the Declaration of Independence. Its county seat was established at Greasy Rock, which was renamed Sneedville in honor of lawyer John L.T. Sneed, who successfully defended the suit brought against the new county.[1]

The first court met at the home of Alexander Campbell. This was followed by the use of the old Union Church. The latter was used until 1850, when a small brick courthouse was erected.[2] This structure was destroyed by fire in 1886.

The next courthouse was a two story brick structure with an open two story entry porch supported by square brick pillars fashioned to match the quoin designs found on the building walls. Stairways were located at each side of the open porch. The porch was further embellished with decorative wood segmental arches at the second floor and complicated scrollwork railings on the second floor balcony and stairways. The building had a hip roof and a small gable over the center of the porch. A tall, square cupola was located in the center of the hip roof.

The current courthouse was completed in 1931. It is of Neo-classical style and was designed by Allen M. Dryden. The building is a two story brick structure with a projecting stone Corinthian order portico and full stone entablature, which extends across the front and around the sides of the building. This courthouse was constructed by the Emery Construction Company.

Hancock County's Victorian courthouse around 1910.

HARDEMAN COUNTY

Formed: October 16, 1823
Formed from: Western District
County seat: Bolivar
Area: 668 sq.mi.

Hardeman County was named for Col. Thomas Jones Hardeman, who served with Andrew Jackson in the War of 1812 and was one of the commissioners who established Bolivar in 1825. The courts met at the home of Thomas McNeal until the selection of Hatchie Town as county seat.[1] Hatchie Town was a trading outpost established in the late 18th century. It was later renamed Bolivar in 1825 in honor of Simon Bolivar, the liberator of Venezuela.

The first courthouse was built of logs on the public square in 1824. The courts were housed on the first floor and the jail on the second. This structure was used until 1827,[2] when it was moved and became the start of Levi Joy's home.

A permanent brick courthouse, with rooms for courts and offices, was completed on the public square in 1827. Bolivar was occupied early during the Civil War. Union General Samuel D. Sturgis ordered the city to be razed in 1864 and all of the downtown area and many homes, including the courthouse, were destroyed in the fire.[3] The courthouse records, however, were saved.

The current courthouse, Hardeman County's third, was completed in 1868 on the site of the second courthouse. This two story brick structure was designed by Willis, Sloan, and Trigg, architects and builders of Bolivar.[4] The building was financed by a $25,000 bond issue. The design features a handsome Corinthian order pedimented portico set on a rusticated stone base. A square bell and clock tower was also placed in the center of the roof. In 1955 three story brick wings were added to each side of the courthouse.

Left: The Joy-Hardaway House, used as Hardeman County's first courthouse. Right: An early 1870s photo of the current courthouse. In the background are the Bolivar Hotel (left) and Bolivar Opera House (right).

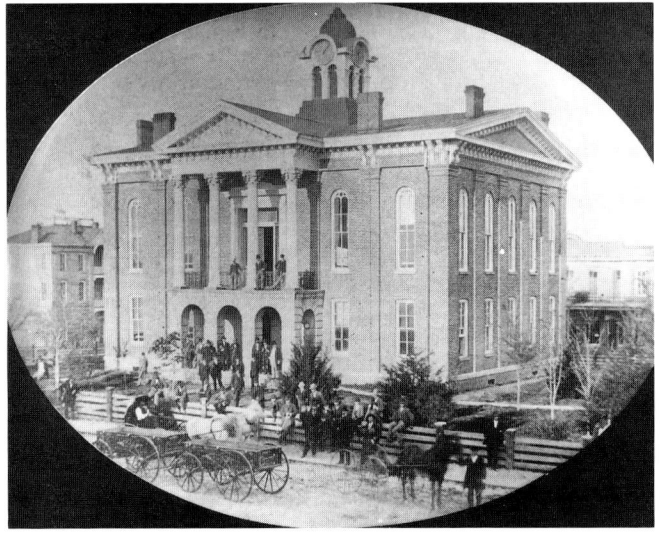

HARDIN COUNTY

Formed: November 13, 1819
Formed from: Western District
County seat: Savannah
Area: 578 sq.mi.

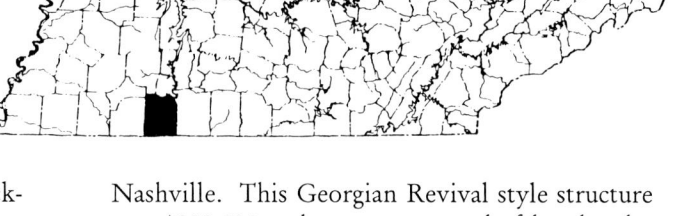

Hardin County was named for Colonel Joseph Hardin of Roane County, a veteran in the Revolutionary War. The first courthouse was built for $30.00 in 1820 by John G. Williams at Hardinsville. This was a small 16 x 20 foot log building with a dirt floor and a clapboard roof.[1] It was followed by a new courthouse, the county seat's only brick structure, around 1823. James Barnes has been credited with the building of this next courthouse.[2]

The county seat was moved to more centrally located Savannah in 1830. Here a temporary log courthouse was constructed east of the present courthouse site. A brick courthouse was completed in 1832, functioning until it was destroyed by fire during the Civil War.

The next courthouse, a substantial two story brick structure utilizing brick and stone salvaged from the 1832 structure, was completed in 1867 by Stephen Randolph and Anthony Gholson for $10,000. The design of this structure is reminiscent of earlier East Tennessee courthouses with its recessed entry portico and gable roof. This building served the county well, but fell into disrepair in the early 1900s. It was replaced in 1905.

The next courthouse was completed in 1906. Designed by R.A. Heavner & H.T. McGee of Jackson, it was 100 x 60 feet. This building was constructed of brick on a stone foundation and was two stories high. It had a projecting pedimented two story entry portico at the main entrance and had entrances on the other three sides as well. The low hip roof was surmounted by a central clock tower 85 feet high. This courthouse burned in 1949.[3]

The present courthouse, completed in 1952, was designed by Marr and Holman Architects of Nashville. This Georgian Revival style structure cost $800,000 and was constructed of handmade Virginia brick with Indiana Bedford limestone trim and steps, and has a slate roof. It features a projecting pedimented entry portico and a tall, thin clock tower. Italian marble was used for interior floors, stairs and wall finishes. The roofing slates were from Vermont.[4]

Left: The courthouse completed in 1867. Right: Hardin County's 1906 courthouse.

HAWKINS COUNTY

Formed: 1786
Formed from: Sullivan County, NC
County seat: Rogersville
Area: 487 sq.mi.

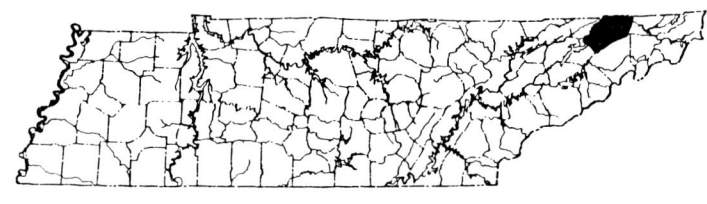

Hawkins County was formed by the state of North Carolina while the State of Franklin was concurrently functioning. It was named for Benjamin Hawkins, a U.S. senator who signed the Deed of Cession conveying the Southwest Territory to the federal government. The designation of Rogersville (named for Joseph Rogers, the first settler at that place) as the county seat was one of the last acts of North Carolina prior to the act of cession in 1789.[1]

Two acres of land were provided by Joseph Rogers for the public buildings. Rogersville was laid out in 1787 and was referred to as Hawkins Courthouse. The first, temporary courthouse was built of logs. It was a one story structure with weatherboarding and was occupied until 1836-37. It was followed by a second courthouse of which nothing appears to be known.

The county commissioners advertised in the Knoxville newspapers for an "undertaker" to build a *house...of brick, on a stone foundation, and covered with tin.* A contract was let to John Dameron of Sullivan County in 1835. While the plan of the building was pre-determined, Dameron was free to design with respect to detailing of the building and the design of the cupola. This third courthouse was a Greek Revival style design, one of the first in the state. Completed in 1836, it was constructed of handmade brick, including the four massive columns.[2]

During the 1870s the interior stairways were removed for additional offices and the stairways were placed outside. The stairways were restored to their original position in 1929. However, Dameron's distinctive cupola was removed and replaced with a New England type church steeple and a large addition was constructed at the rear of the courthouse. This courthouse remains one of six still in use that pre-date the Civil War.

An early 1870s photograph showing the courthouse with its original cupola and the original exterior staircases.

HAYWOOD COUNTY

Formed: November 3, 1823
Formed from: Western District
County seat: Brownsville
Area: 533 sq.mi.

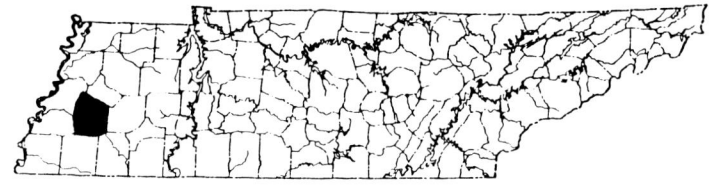

Haywood County was named for Judge John Haywood, an outstanding Tennessee jurist. The first court sessions were held at Richard Nixon's residence.[1] In 1824 Brownsville was selected as the county seat. Land for the county seat was purchased from Thomas Johnson Jr. for $1.00 and the money from the sale of lots was sufficient to erect public buildings. A temporary log courthouse 20 x 29 feet was completed in 1825. It was to have *1 door, 3 windows of 15 lights each with shutters, the door to have a good lock, and the house to be furnished with the necessary benches and tables for the court and jury.*[2]

This was followed in 1826 by a wood frame courthouse building on the public square just south of the first courthouse. By 1832 a new structure was erected in the center of the public square for $4,000 by Joseph Coe. By 1845 this courthouse was considered unsafe. It was taken down and rebuilt in brick at that time. In 1868 a west wing was constructed for $12,000. The wing was used by the Tennessee Supreme Court from 1868 to 1869, when it moved back to Jackson.[3]

The present building underwent extensive repairs in 1928, at which time a two story brick addition was completed. This addition included eight offices on the first floor. The Neo-classical design of the courthouse features a recessed entry with two story stone Corinthian columns and a full stone entablature.

A view of the courthouse c1899.

HENDERSON COUNTY

Formed: November 7, 1821
Formed from: Western District
County seat: Lexington
Area: 520 sq.mi.

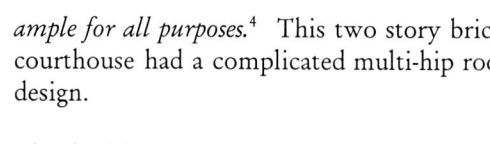

Henderson County was named for Colonel James Henderson who commanded the Tennessee troops at the Battle of New Orleans. Its county seat, Lexington, was named after Lexington, MA. The first court met in the home of Samuel Wilson.

Four acres of land were reserved as a public square in the center of the county seat and around 1822 a one story log courthouse was constructed for $142. This was replaced in 1827 by a two story brick structure built by Samuel Wilson for $4,595.97. This was not considered to be a good building and it was remodelled in 1832-33 by James Baker for $1,000.[1]

The building was again remodelled in 1844 by James Watson, during which time the courts met in the Masonic hall. This structure continued in use until 1863, when it was accidentally burned by the Third Michigan Cavalry who were quartered there.[2]

A third courthouse was constructed in 1867 by Robert Dyer for $7,450. This was a two story brick structure with offices on the first floor and a large courtroom on the second. It had an unusual double, parallel gable roof design. The building burned in 1895.[3]

A fourth courthouse was completed in 1896. Built by B.M. Nelson of Decatur, AL for $11,600 it was considered to be able to meet the county's demands for years to come. It was described as ... *handsome, commodious, and practically fireproof. Each of the county officials are provided with fire proof vaults in connection with the room assigned them. The building is of red pressed brick with stone trimming, a splendid slate roof, a four-faced clock. The circuit court room is seated with opera chairs and ceiled with steel and the county court room is ample for all purposes.*[4] This two story brick courthouse had a complicated multi-hip roof design.

This building was replaced in 1961 for a cost of $500,000 by the county's fifth courthouse. Hart, Freeland, Roberts of Nashville were the architects.

Left: The 1867 courthouse. Right: Henderson County's fourth courthouse.

HENRY COUNTY

Formed: November 11, 1821
Formed from: Western District
County seat: Paris
Area: 562 sq.mi.

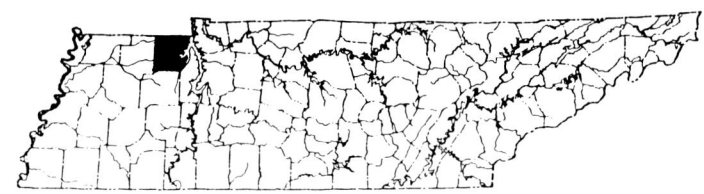

Henry County was named in honor of Patrick Henry, Revolution patriot and governor of Virginia. The first court session was held at the home of Peter Wall. Paris was laid out as the county seat in 1823[1] (this name was apparently selected because of the popularity of the Marquis de Lafayette at that time). Land was then sold to defray the cost of public buildings, with four acres reserved for the public square.[2]

The first courthouse was built in 1823. It was a two room structure built of poplar logs. This was replaced in 1825 by a two story brick courthouse built by John Burke and Francis McConnell for $123. In 1833 the county added several off-site office locations for additional space.[3] A third courthouse, built in 1852, was larger and more imposing. It was built by Calvin Sweeney for $42,000 and served until 1897.[4]

The current, fourth courthouse was completed in 1897 and was designed by architect Reuben H. Hunt of Chattanooga. The design is similar to that of Hunt and Lamb's courthouse design for Bradley County.[5] This two story brick structure is trimmed with stone and features an arched principal entrance. The roof is a complicated hip design with corner pyramidal roofs and dormers as well as a tall clock tower and cupola rising above the main entrance. The builder was E.M. Wallen.

Left: Early 20th cntury view of the completed courthouse. Right: The current courthouse under construction.

HICKMAN COUNTY

Formed: December 3, 1807
Formed from: Dickson County
County seat: Centerville
Area: 613 sq.mi.

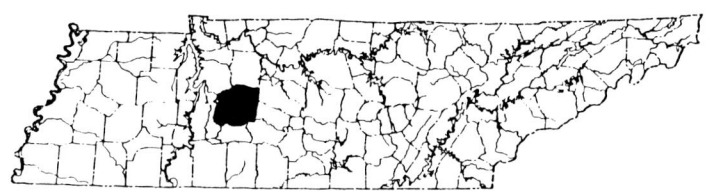

Hickman County was named for Edmund Hickman, a surveyor killed on the Duck River by Indians. By 1810 the county seat was established at Vernon, eight miles west of Centerville, and a log courthouse was erected. The county seat was moved to Centerville in 1823 and the logs from the old building were reused for the new courthouse. A brick courthouse was erected in 1825. This structure was enlarged in 1849. It was burned in 1864 during the Civil War to prevent its further use as a fort by the Federal troops.

The next courthouse was completed in 1867 at a cost of $10,000. It was a two story brick structure with the county offices on the first floor and the courtroom on the second.[1] The design of this structure was similar to several earlier East Tennesssee courthouses, with its recessed portico topped by a simple pedimented gable. Within the portico was an open staircase to the second floor. At each end of the standing seam metal gable roof are double chimneys. This structure was torn down in 1926.

The current courthouse, Hickman County's fifth, was completed in 1926. Tisdale, Pinson, and Stone of Nashville were the architects. This is a two story brick structure with a full basement.

The facade features engaged two story pilasters and arched windows on the second floor.

Hickman County's fourth courthouse (1867).

HOUSTON COUNTY

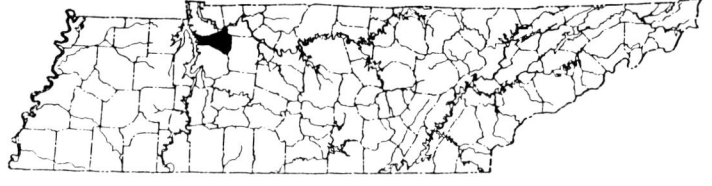

Formed: January 21, 1871
Formed from: Dickson, Humphreys, and Stewart Counties
County seat: Erin
Area: 200 sq.mi.

Houston County was named in honor of Sam Houston, Tennessee congressman and governor. The first county court was held at the Union Church in Erin. Arlington was initially selected as the county seat, and a courthouse was completed there in 1872. This contract was awarded to G.W. Buquo, who built a wood frame structure for $1,440.[1] This structure is now in use as the Arlington Cumberland Presbyterian Church.

An election in 1878 resulted in the county seat being moved to Erin where the courts were held on the second floor of Jacob Buquo's store. In 1882, a two story brick courthouse was completed for $7,000. Stone was used for the foundation as well as for a belt course to separate the first and second stories. The combination gable and hip roof was topped by a square cupola around which ran an iron railing. Four entrances opened into a large cross hallway.[2] Offices were located on the first floor with the courtroom occupying the entire second floor. L.J. Neville was the architect and builder of this courthouse, which stood until 1956 when it was dismantled for the construction of a new structure.

The current Houston County courthouse was designed by Burkhalter-Hickerson & Associates architects of Nashville. A two story brick structure trimmed with stone, this courthouse cost $185,000.

Left: The Arlington Cumberland Presbyterian Church now occupies the first courthouse. The exterior of this wood frame structure has been covered with brick. Right: The second Houston County Courthouse (1882).

HUMPHREYS COUNTY

Formed: October 19, 1809
Formed from: Smith and Steward Counties
County seat: Waverly
Area: 532 sq.mi.

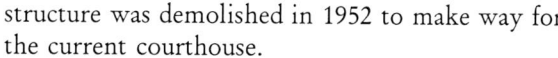

Humphreys County was named for Perry W. Humphreys, Superior Court judge and congressman. The first court was held at the home of Samuel Parker Jr. on Trace Creek two miles west of Waverly. The county seat was established in 1816 at Reynoldsburg, named for John B. Reynolds, then a representative in congress.

The courthouse erected at Reynoldsburg, completed in 1812, was a two story brick structure, 30 feet square. The lower story was fitted out with a courtroom and office while the second floor contained three small offices.[1] With the removal of the county seat to Waverly in 1835, this structure was purchased by Major T.K. Wyly for use as a residence.[2]

Waverly (named for Sir Walter Scott's Waverly novels) was surveyed and laid out in 1837. A large two story brick courthouse was erected, similar in design to the courthouse at Reynoldsburg for $6,000. It was destroyed by fire in 1876.[3]

The second courthouse at Waverly, completed in 1878 at a cost of $16,000, was a large two story brick structure on a stone foundation. It had four offices and two halls on the first floor and a court room, lobby, and gallery on the second. The building was provided with four main entrances, had a tin covered gable roof and was designed by St. Louis architect P. J. Pauley. This structure was destroyed by fire in 1898.[4]

The third courthouse, completed in 1899 cost $15,000 and was a large, handsome two story brick and stone Neo-classical style structure. This courthouse design featured engaged classical pilasters, stone window lintels, and a strong classical cornice at the roof level with a pediment over the principal entrance. It was finished with a low hipped roof with a central square cupola. The structure was demolished in 1952 to make way for the current courthouse.

Humphrey County's current courthouse is its fifth and was built for $190,000. It was designed by Steinbaugh and Wheeler, Architects.

Left: The courthouse erected at Reynoldsburg. Right: The 1899 Humphreys County Courthouse.

JACKSON COUNTY

Formed: November 6, 1801
Formed from: Smith County
County seat: Gainesboro
Area: 309 sq.mi.

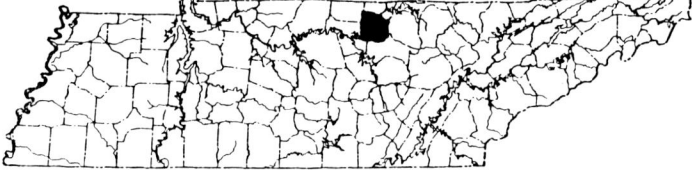

Jackson County was named in honor of Andrew Jackson, who was at that time a Superior Court judge. The first court was held at the home of John Bowen on Roaring River. The town of Smithfield was proposed as county seat; however, the town did not develop as hoped because it was difficult to get to and there was more settlement on the west side of the county. For a brief period the courts were held at Benjamin Blackburn's fort at Double Springs.[1]

Williamsburg was selected as county seat in 1806, and a brick courthouse was built there. 60 acres were laid out, with two acres reserved in the center for the courthouse. This courthouse was built by William White, who also built the jail.[2]

The county seat was eventually moved to Gainesboro, named for General Edmund Pendleton Gaines, following an election in 1817. The courts were held in a private house in the community of Old Columbus until the new courthouse was completed. This courthouse was built with the proceeds of the sale of lots and was a square two story brick structure with a gable roof. The courthouse burned in August 14, 1874. By tradition, this courthouse was built by a Mr. Haney, who also built the first house in Gainesboro.[3]

A third courthouse, completed in 1874, was built by David L. Dow and served until 1903, when it was determined to be unsafe and was demolished. This was a three story brick and stone structure with a low hipped roof and central square domed cupola. Stepped gables were located at the roof line above each of the four entrance pavilions. Low pyramid roofed pavilions were located in each corner.

The next courthouse was built on the foundations of the previous courthouse at a cost of $17,500. It stood until destroyed by fire in 1926. Until a new courthouse could be completed, the court house and jail activities were temporarily located in a store at 200 East Hull.[4]

The current courthouse, Jackson County's fifth, was completed in 1927. It is a three story brick structure with handsome limestone trim designed in a Neo-classical revival style by Tisdale, Pinson, and Stone Architects of Nashville. The design features a tall square clock tower.

Left: The second Jackson County Courthouse. Right: The third courthouse, completed in 1874.

JEFFERSON COUNTY

Formed: June 11, 1792
Formed from: Greene and Hawkins Counties
County seat: Dandridge
Area: 274 sq.mi.

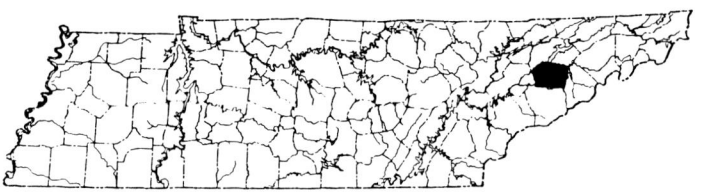

Jefferson County was named in honor of Thomas Jefferson. The first court was held at the home of Jeremiah Matthews. Dandridge was selected as the county seat in 1793 and was named after Martha Dandridge Custis Washington, wife of George Washington. Dandridge claims to be the second oldest city in the state.

According to the Goodspeed histories, *the character of the first county buildings erected in Dandridge is not known, but they were undoubtedly like those of other counties at that time, rude log structures.... The courthouse remembered by the oldest residents was a small brick structure standing on the lower side of the present lot.*[1]

The first courts were held in the residence of Jeremiah Matthews, four miles west of Dandridge on July 23, 1792. Later courts were held a few times across the street from the present courthouse in a building later known as the Sanders House. The first courthouse, built in the 1790s and used until 1845, was a small brick building near the current courthouse. It was torn down.[2]

Planning for the existing courthouse was begun in 1840. Construction of this building was completed in 1845 by the Hickman Brothers[3]. It apparently took several years because of various delays. The current courthouse is a two story brick structure with a recessed two story portico and a tall tower. The courthouse originally had four offices and a courtroom on the first floor and four offices and a large auditorium on the second. Two curving stairways originally led to the second floor and auditorium ("Thespian Hall"), which was used for public functions. The final cost was $6,666.00.[4] During the Civil War the auditorium was used as a hospital. It was later converted to offices. In the late 1950s offices, vaults and restrooms were added at a cost of $125,000. During the 1970s the courthouse was restored.[5]

Left: The earliest photo of the courthouse showing 16-over-16 windows and shutters. Center: A c1900 photo showing the windows changed to 4-over-4 and the shutters removed. Right: An early view of this structure from the rear.

JOHNSON COUNTY

Formed: January 2, 1836
Formed from: Carter County
County seat: Mountain City
Area: 299 sq.mi.

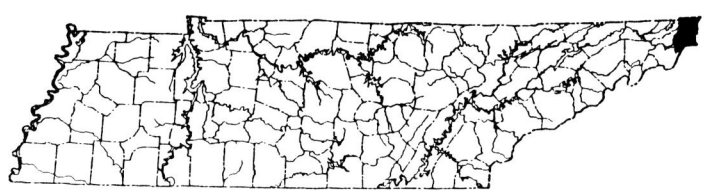

Johnson County was named for Thomas Johnson, an early settler. Johnson's house was used for the court sessions until a courthouse could be constructed. The county seat was established at Taylorsville, named for Nathaniel Taylor, a pioneer settler. The name was changed to Mountain City in 1885.

The first courthouse was completed in 1837. It was a two story structure, 40 feet square. This building was used until it was declared unsafe in 1894 and was torn down.[1]

The second courthouse, in use until 1958, was a two story brick structure with a one story covered entry porch over its principal entrance. The second floor contained the courtroom, which was marked by tall arched windows and decorative brick bands. The courthouse had a cross-gable roof and a center square cupola with a bell-shaped roof.

The third, current courthouse was completed at a cost of $225,000. It is a modern two story brick, glass and stone structure completed in 1958.

The second Johnson County Courthouse, 1894.

KNOX COUNTY

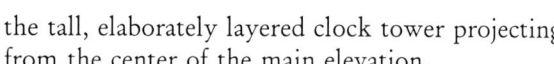

Formed: June 11, 1792
Formed from: Greene and Hawkins Counties
County seat: Knoxville
Area: 509 sq.mi.

Knox County was named for General Henry Knox, the Secretary of War in Washington's cabinet. Knoxville was founded and laid out in 1791 and became the state capital in 1796, when Tennessee became the 16th state in the Union. The county court met initially at the house of John Stone in Knoxville.[1]

Temporary buildings were erected for the courthouse and jail around 1792. These were destroyed soon after by a fire set by a lawyer. Until a new courthouse was erected seven years later, the courts met in a building rented from Col. James White. A new two story courthouse, 30 by 40 feet, was erected in 1797 at a cost of $5,803.19 and was described as being *...built of rough fragments of rock cemented with mortar, and did not present a very handsome exterior.*[2]

In 1839 the county commission met to review the condition of the old courthouse and decided to build a new structure. This structure, costing $9,570, was tendered in 1842, but was not immediately accepted as it had not been completed according to the agreement. It was a two story brick structure with a center recessed pedimented portico, a style which appears to have been the basis for numerous other courthouse designs in the state. In the center of its gable roof was a square cupola. Barnes Crawford of Knoxville was the builder-contractor for this structure. A dome with bell and clock was added in 1849.[3]

The current, handsome Victorian courthouse, Knox County's fourth, was completed in 1886. Stephenson and Getaz were the architects. It is a large two story brick structure elaborately trimmed in stone and is set on a tall basement. Upon completion it cost $136,000. On the first floor were the criminal and county courtrooms as well as grand jury and witness-rooms and office. Additional offices were located on the second floor.[4] Unusual among Tennessee courthouse designs is the tall, elaborately layered clock tower projecting from the center of the main elevation.

The courthouse has had several additions over the years, including a modern adjacent city-county annex building which faces the river and is connected to the original courthouse. This was completed in 1979 and was designed by the City-County Building Associated Architects (Lindsay & Maples and McCarty Hosaple McCarty, J/V) of Knoxville.

Left: Knox County's 1842 courthouse. Right: The 1886 courthouse prior to later additions.

LAKE COUNTY

Formed: June 9, 1870
Formed from: Obion County
County seat: Tiptonville
Area: 163 sq.mi.

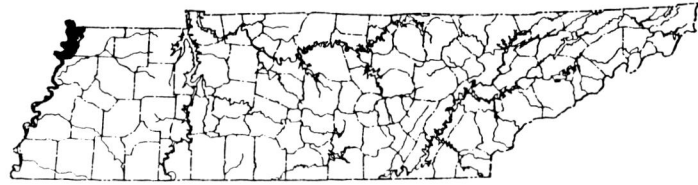

Lake County was named for Reelfoot Lake, which was formed by a series of earthquakes in 1811 that dammed the Reelfoot River and caused changes in the course of the Mississippi River. The first county court was held at the Athenaeum Hall in Tiptonville, which was selected as the county seat on September 5, 1870.

Tiptonville, also known as the "town on wheels," was rebuilt twice. It was initially destroyed by Federal gunboats during the Civil War. After that, the town was "swallowed" by the Mississippi River and was rebuilt on higher ground.[1]

One acre was donated for the courthouse, but the county magistrates instead purchased the Athenaeum. (This building was later moved to a location in the J.C. Harris subdivision.)[2]

The first (and current) courthouse constructed in Tiptonville was a wood frame structure. It was completed in 1905. The handsome original design featured a projecting two story entry pavilion with a porch over the front entrance, a bay window on the side and a tall hip roof with a square cupola and dormers.

In 1936 it was extensively renovated, which resulted in the building being encased in brick. The WPA renovation was completed by H.J. McGuire & Co., of Memphis for $90,000.[3] This renovation completely changed the appearance of the courthouse. In addition to the brick and stone veneer, a two story porch with pillars was added on the front and additional offices and a vault were added to the rear. The courtroom was also completely remodelled and the interior was replastered and painted.

A major fire in July 1989 resulted in substantial damage to the building. This was, however, repaired and the building was reoccupied in the Spring of 1990.

A view of the original courthouse design taken in December 1907.

LAUDERDALE COUNTY

Formed: November 24, 1835
Formed from: Dyer and Tipton Counties
County seat: Ripley
Area: 471 sq.mi.

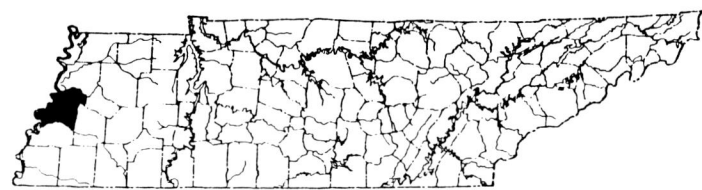

Lauderdale County was named in honor of Col. James Lauderdale, who was killed leading a charge of his regiment of Tennessee troops in the Battle of New Orleans. The first circuit court met in the home of Col. Jacob Byler, while the first county court was held at the home of Samuel Lusk. Both homes were outside of Ripley,[1] the county seat. Ripley was named for General Ripley, a veteran of the war of 1812.

By 1836 a temporary courthouse, 22 by 26 feet and 17 feet high, had been constructed for $200.[2]

This structure was used until 1844, when a new frame courthouse was constructed on the public square at a cost of $4,000. This courthouse burned in 1869.

The next courthouse, completed in 1870, was a two story brick structure built at a cost of $20,000.[3] It was nearly square in plan and the window bays were outlined by full height raised brick panels. This structure had a low hipped roof. It was demolished in 1935.

The current courthouse was completed in 1936 and was designed by Marr and Holman of Nashville. Funded in part by the Federal Public Works Administration, this structure cost $120,000. It is a brick building trimmed with stone and features Art Deco detailing.

Left: The 1870 courthouse. Center: A c1912 interior view of the courtroom. Right: A mid-20th century postcard view of the current county courthouse.

LAWRENCE COUNTY

Formed: October 21, 1817
Formed from: Hickman and Maury Counties
County seat: Lawrenceburg
Area: 617 sq.mi.

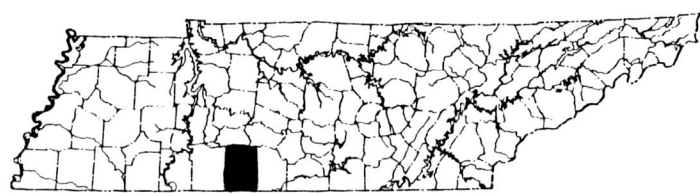

Lawrence County was named in honor of Capt. James Lawrence, who commanded the "Chesapeake" during the War of 1812 and is famous for his command, "Don't give up the ship." The first court was held in the home of Dr. Joseph Farmer. In 1819, a temporary log courthouse 25 feet square was constructed at Jonesboro.

Following the establishment of Lawrenceburg as the county seat in 1821, a two story brick courthouse, also 25 feet square, was constructed. This was known as the "David Crockett Courthouse" in honor of one of the county's first settlers. By 1847, a decision was made to repair and add to the courthouse for $2,350. At that time the height of the building was increased by two feet. In 1850, the Freemasons and Odd Fellows added an additional story at their own expense ($1,500).[1] This new construction was topped with a low hipped roof and a small bell tower cupola. Union forces threatened to burn the courthouse during the Civil War, but Major Gibbons was persuaded not to do so. The courthouse was repaired in 1866 and its cupola was removed in 1867.

By 1905 the county decided that a new courthouse was necessary. The old building was sold for $255. The design of architect W. Chamberlain & Co. was accepted. Built by M. T. Lewman & Co. of Louisville, KY, the courthouse was completed in January of 1906 at a cost of $29,639.06. This was a two story brick structure with octagonal corner towers. The central section had a hipped roof with an octagonal clock tower.[2]

Part of a major urban renewal plan, the current courthouse was completed in 1974 at a cost of $1,100,000. It was designed by Hart, Freeland, Roberts, Architects of Nashville.

Left: The "David Crockett" courthouse with its full three stories and bell tower. Right: The 1905 Lawrence County courthouse.

LEWIS COUNTY

Formed: December 23, 1843
Formed from: Hickman Lawrence, Maury and Wayne Counties
County seat: Hohenwald
Area: 282 sq.mi.

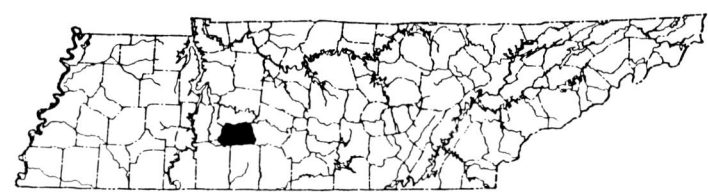

Lewis County was named in honor of Merriwether Lewis, captain in the Army of the United States, secretary to President Jefferson, and later co-commander of the Lewis & Clark Expedition to the Pacific Northwest. The first county courts were held at various residences. A log courthouse was built in 1846 at Gordon, the first county seat, which was named for Powhattan Gordon of Columbia, TN.

In 1848 the county seat and log courthouse were moved to Newburg. This courthouse was demolished in 1857 and replaced with a two story frame structure, 40 by 40 feet. This structure was completed for $1,500 and had a courtroom on the first floor and county offices on the second.[1] Extremely simple in design, it had tall, narrow windows and a hip roof with a square cupola in the center.

In 1897 the county seat was moved a third time, to Hohenwald (meaning "high forest"). This name was given by a colony of enterprising Swiss settlers. A courthouse was completed here in that year.

This courthouse was replaced in 1939, in part funded by the Federal Public Works Administration. Niles Yearwood of Nashville was the contractor. This simple two story brick structure has a tall central block flanked by lower two story wings.

A view of the 1857 courthouse at Newburg.

LINCOLN COUNTY

Formed: November 14, 1809
Formed from: Bedford County
County seat: Fayetteville
Area: 570 sq.mi.

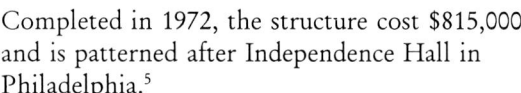

Lincoln County was named for Major General Benjamin Lincoln of the Revolutionary War era. The first court met at the home of Brice M. Garner. The commission members were charged with building a *temporary courthouse on the public square as near the center as the brick house already let will admit of to be, 18 feet by 20 feet, in the clear round logs, with a good cabin roof...The house to be built ready for the setting of the May Court.* Built by James Fuller for $35, this structure consisted of one room, had a wood floor, and was completed on May 29, 1811.[1]

This was soon followed by a new two story brick structure on the square, built by Micajah and William McElroy for $3,472.63-1/2.[2] The specifications for this courthouse still survive. It describes the building as being 40 feet square, with a stone foundation and two story brick walls. Fireplaces were located in each corner of the second floor, which was accessed by a stairs in the northwest corner.[3] This building was abused during the Civil War, being used as a stable, housing and protection for the troops.[4]

In 1872 it was decided to replace the courthouse and a third courthouse was begun in 1873. This was a brick structure 60 by 80 feet, with all of the county offices on the first floor and the courtroom on the second floor. The budget for this courthouse was $30,000 and W.T. Moyers, J. A. Albright, and W. E. Turley were the contractors, completing the building in 1874.

The current courthouse was designed by Morton-Carter and Associates of Nashville and was built by Shepherd Construction Co., also of Nashville. Completed in 1972, the structure cost $815,000 and is patterned after Independence Hall in Philadelphia.[5]

Two views of the 1874 courthouse. Left: An 1886 view taken during a debate between Robert L. Taylor and Alfred A. Taylor. Right: A c1930 view.

LOUDON COUNTY

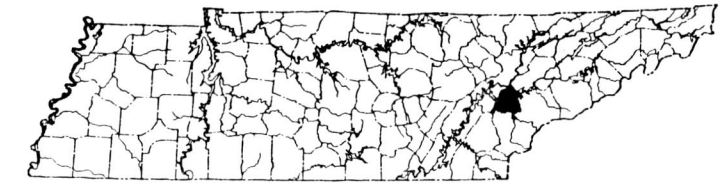

Formed: May 27, 1870
Formed from: Blount, McMinn, Monroe, and Roane Counties
County seat: Loudon
Area: 229 sq.mi.

Loudon County was named in honor of Fort Loudoun, erected by the British in 1756 and named for the Earl of Loudoun, commander-in-chief of British and American colonial troops in the Southern Colonies during the French and Indian War.

Loudon County has had only one courthouse. It was built on the town square site, donated for this purpose. Construction began in 1871 and was completed in September 1872. This courthouse was built by J. Wesley Clarke & Brothers for $14,200 to the design of architect A.C. Bruce of Knoxville.[1]

A late example of the Italianate style, this handsome two story brick structure is composed of a tall central two story section with lower two story wings. Entry doors are paired on the central block, and single doors are found on either side. The facade is enriched by brick piers which are rusticated on the first story, as well as a decorative horizontal band between the first and second storys, and corbelled brickwork beneath the end gables and center pediment. A deep bracketed cornice is located at the roof eave. The central section has a low hip roof which is topped by a square central cupola. The wings have gable roofs. The exterior appears only to have undergone minor changes. These include the removal of the shutters from the first floor windows and the replacement of the original roof of the cupola.

An early 20th century view of the Loudon County courthouse showing its original cupola design, first floor shutters and Victorian-era paint scheme.

MACON COUNTY

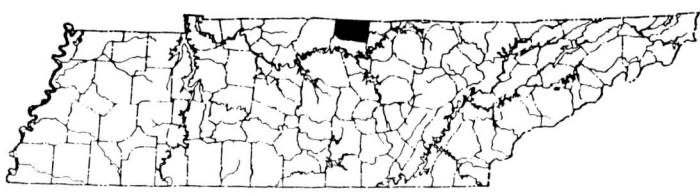

Formed: January 18, 1842
Formed from: Smith and Sumner Counties
County seat: Lafayette
Area: 307 sq.mi.

Macon County was named for Nathaniel Macon of North Carolina, a U.S. representative and later senator from that state. The first courts were held in the home of William Dunn.[1] Lafayette was named the county seat in 1842 and the first courthouse was constructed in 1844. This was a two story brick structure, forty feet square, built at a cost of $4,000. The courtroom was located on the first floor and there was a jury room and two offices on the second. This structure was destroyed by fire in 1860.[2]

A second courthouse was begun in 1861, but construction was interrupted by the Civil War and this structure was not completed until 1866. Also a two story brick structure, 40 by 52 feet, it cost $10,000. The first floor had four offices, a main hallway and stairs, while the second contained the courtroom and two jury rooms. It also burned in 1901.[3]

The third courthouse was completed at a cost of $10,800. It was a two story brick and stone structure, fifty feet square, and featured a tall domed corner clock tower. The first floor elevation included strong horizontal bands with flat arched windows. The second floor windows had round arched tops. Stepped gables were located over each entrance and the low hip roof was augmented by low pyramid roofs at three corners. Large offices were located in the corners on both floors. A winding staircase led to the second floor floor courtroom, which had a balcony. In 1932 this structure was destroyed by fire.[4]

The current courthouse, Macon County's fourth, was completed in 1933 at a cost of $16,000 by E. Tate & Son, a Nashville contractor. The courthouse was renovated in the 1970s.

Macon County's third courthouse.

MADISON COUNTY

Formed: November 11, 1821
Formed from: The Western District
County seat: Jackson
Area: 557 sq.mi.

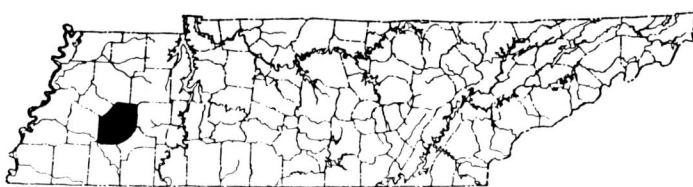

Madison County was named in honor of James Madison, fourth president of the United States. Jackson was selected as county seat in 1822 and was named in honor of Andrew Jackson, the seventh president. The first courts met at A.R. Alexander's home at Golden Station until the September 1822 term.[1]

The first courthouse, a log structure covered with clapboards, was built on the northeast corner of the public square. It was completed in 1822 at a cost of $135. This structure was 30 by 40 feet, had a dirt floor, a judge's bench and door of hewn lumber, and a chimney built of logs and mud.[2]

The second courthouse was a two story brick structure completed in 1824 by Benjamin Gholson. In addition to the courthouse, offices for the county court clerk and registry office were erected at the northeast corner and for the circuit court clerk at the southwest corner of the square.[3] The courthouse was also used as a church as there were not yet any in the town.

Planning began for a third courthouse in 1837. It was completed in 1839 and was a two story brick structure built at a cost of $25,000 by Thomas Brown. This courthouse, 50 by 60 feet in plan, was a two story brick structure with a raised two-story pilaster and panel design on the exterior. In the center of the low hip roof was an domed octagonal cupola. This courthouse contained rooms for all county offices and a room for the various county courts as well as a supreme court room. It was extensively remodelled in 1848[4] and was again cleaned out and repaired in 1865, following the Civil War.

The next courthouse was completed in 1907.[5] It was a large, two story brick structure with a tall pyramidal roofed clock tower over the front of the building. The tower roof also incorporated a complicated arrangement of dormers and corner turrets. The main roof was a combination of both hips and gables together with tall chimneys. This courthouse continued in use until 1937.

The current courthouse, Madison County's fifth, was completed in 1937. The architects were Marr and Holman of Nashville. Completed at a cost of $300,000, it was partially funded by the federal Public Works Administration. The exterior of the building consists of Indiana limestone, while Tennessee marble is used on the interior.

Left: Madison County's third courthouse (1837). Right: The fourth courthouse completed in 1907.

MARION COUNTY

Formed: November 20, 1817
Formed from: Cherokee lands
County seat: Jasper
Area: 500 sq.mi.

Marion County was named in honor of Brigadier General Francis Marion, the Revolutionary War leader in South Carolina known as the "Swamp Fox." The county seat, Jasper, was named for Sergeant William Jasper, a Revolutionary War hero. The early county courts met at the Cheek residence in Whitwell. The county seat was moved to Jasper in 1823, at which time a brick courthouse was constructed by John Mathas. This was a four-square structure, used from 1824 to 1879.[1]

A larger two story brick courthouse was constructed in 1880. This structure was of Second Empire style and featured a central gable roofed projecting pavilion, tall arched windows, mansard roofs and a central cupola. It was built by John Jones and was used until it burned in 1922, at which time many records were lost.

The present two story brick courthouse, the county's third, was completed in 1925. It is a two story brick structure of Neo-classical design incorporating arched windows, two story Doric pilasters, projecting end pavilions and a full entablature at roof level. The courthouse was damaged by fire in 1984 and was renovated in 1986 by Warren Construction of Shelbyville, TN.

Left: The architect's sketch for the second courthouse Center: The second courthouse as completed (1880). Right: The current courthouse prior to the 1984 fire.

MARSHALL COUNTY

Formed: February 26, 1836
Formed from: Bedford, Giles, Lincoln, and Maury Counties
County seat: Lewisburg
Area: 375 sq.mi.

Marshall County was named in honor of John Marshall of Virginia, member of congress, Secretary of State, and Chief Justice of the United States from 1801-1835. The county seat, Lewisburg, was incorporated in 1837 and was named for Merriweather Lewis, co-commander of the Lewis and Clark Expedition to the Pacific Northwest.

The county's first courthouse was constructed in 1836 in the center of the public square. It was a two story brick structure with a a center cupola on its roof. Modelled on the courthouse at Shelbyville, it was about sixty feet square and cost $8,750. The north and south entries were emphasized by porticoes and wrought iron balconies at the second floor. The first floor had cross hallways with one large office in each corner. Stairs went up the north side of the east/west hall. The courtroom was located on the north side of the second floor while two offices were located on the south side.[1] This building was destroyed by fire in 1872.

A second courthouse was completed in 1874 at a cost of $21,000. This was also a two story brick structure of similar design to the previous courthouse. It was rectangular in plan, had a pedimented gabled roof with a central square clock tower, and projecting two story pedimented projecting porticoes on each of its long sides. In 1927 this courthouse also burned.

The current courthouse was designed by the Nashville architectural firm of Hart, Freeland, and Roberts. It was completed in 1929 at a cost of $125,000. The same firm was employed in the renovation of the structure in 1974 which cost $377,407.69.

Left: The second Marshall County courthouse (1874). Right: A view of the current courthouse in 1931.

MAURY COUNTY

Formed: November 24, 1807
Formed from: Williamson County
County seat: Columbia
Area: 613 sq.mi.

Maury County was named in honor of Abram Maury, a Williamson County surveyor appointed to lay out the counties in West Tennessee. The first court met at the home of Joseph Brown, three miles south of Columbia, until a log courthouse was completed in 1808. Columbia was established as the county seat and the public sale of lots in 1808 was used to raise money to build the first public buildings.

The second, permanent courthouse was built by Osborn P. Nicholson and John M. Goodloe in 1810. It was 30 by 60 feet, of brick construction, and had a cornice and cupola.[1] Completed in 1811, this structure cost $6,900. By 1844 a decision had been made to build a new courthouse. The second courthouse was sold for $10. However, the man failed to tear down this structure, described by Nathan Vaught as a *...shanty of a courthouse on the east side of the public square...*, as it was too well constructed.

The next courthouse was begun in 1846. The contract was awarded to Nimrod Porter and the construction cost was not to exceed $15,000. The plans and specifications for this structure were prepared by William Watkins, who also superintended the construction. The final cost was $19,170 and the building was not completed until late 1847. This structure was 87 by 49 feet, with a floor to ceiling heights of nine, 13, and 11 on the first, second and third floors, respectively. On the exterior, full height brick pilasters lined the walls of this low hip roof structure. In 1859 a committee investigated adding four porticos and a cupola to this structure. It was demolished in 1903 to make way for the current courthouse.[2]

The county's present, fourth courthouse, was completed in 1906 to architectural designs by Carpenter and Blair of New York (J. Edwin Carpenter, born in Columbia, was the first native Tennessean to receive formal architectural training.[3]) The courthouse cost $120,000 and is in the Beaux Arts style. The design includes a tall central cupola. In 1973 the courthouse was remodelled by Howard, Nielson, Lyne, Batey, and O'Brian, Inc. at a cost of $236,000.

Left: The 1847 Maury County Courthouse. Right: An early 20th century view of the current courthouse.

McMINN COUNTY

Formed: November 18, 1819
Formed from: Cherokee lands, Hiwassee District
County seat: Athens
Area: 430 sq.mi.

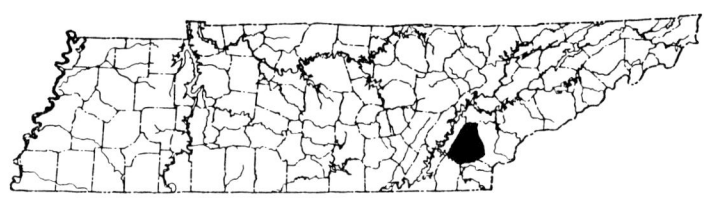

McMinn County was named in honor of Joseph McMinn, member of the state constitutional convention and Governor of Tennessee. The first circuit court was held at the home of Major John Walker in Calhoun in 1820. Here, a temporary log courthouse was erected and used until December 1823, when the courts moved to Athens.[1]

Athens (originally named Pumpkintown) was designated the county seat in 1823.[2] In Athens, the courts used existing buildings until a two story brick courthouse was completed in 1828 on the public square. This structure was 40 by 46 feet.

In 1875 a new courthouse was completed to designs by Knoxville architect A.C. Bruce at a cost of $30,000.[3] This structure was constructed by Thomas and William Cleage (who at one time held contracts for nine other East Tennessee courthouses). A handsome Second Empire style design, this was also a two story brick and stone structure with numerous pavilions projecting from the central block. The windows had elaborate hood moldings, stone quoins were used at the corners, and the roof contained a variety of gables and mansard roofs around the perimeter of the main low hip. In the center stood a tall square clock tower. This courthouse burned in 1964 as it was being renovated.

It was replaced by the present building, McMinn County's fourth courthouse. The structure constructed is a contemporary classically-inspired design by architects Galloway and Guthrie of Knoxville. Featuring a six-column projecting pedimented entry portico and tall clock tower, it was completed at a cost of $750,000.[4]

Left: McMinn County's third courthouse (1875). Right: The architect's original sketch for the third courthouse.

McNAIRY COUNTY

Formed: October 8, 1823
Formed from: Hardin County
County seat: Selmer
Area: 560 sq.mi.

McNairy County was named for John McNairy, judge of the District Court of the United States for Tennessee. The first courts were held in the home of Abel V. Maury in 1824. The original county seat was located at Purdy, where an 18 by 20 foot log cabin was constructed for use as a courthouse in 1825. Purdy was named for Col. John Purdy a surveyor from Henderson County.[1]

In 1830 a brick courthouse was built by James Reed and Ruben Walker (carpenters) and Henry Kirkland (mason). This two story brick structure stood at the north end of the town ...*on the outside of the curving street connecting the two long streets*. It had a low gable roof with a square cupola in the center as well as open porches in the center of both the first and second floors. This courthouse burned in 1881.[2]

The citizens of Purdy successfully resisted efforts of the Mobile and Ohio Railroad to build through their town. This, unfortunately, resulted in a gradual decline and the eventual moving of the county seat to Selmer in 1890. A courthouse was given to the county by P.H. Thrasher to facilitate this move.[3] Begun in 1891, this was a handsome two story brick structure with a tower. The design incorporated projecting pedimented gabled pavilions on each side and a one story projecting porch over the principal entry. Elaborate brick corbelling was used to outline the roof line as well as each of the gables. A tall, square tower was located in the center of the roof. This structure was demolished in 1946.

The present courthouse, the second in Selmer and the county's fourth, was completed in 1949. Marr and Holman of Nashville were the architects. It is a two story stone clad structure, rectangular in form with slightly lower one-bay wide two story wings flanking the colonnade-like principal elevation. The design is an excellent example of the severely restrained Neo-classical design style adopted by that firm.

Left: McNairy County's third courthouse, the first in Selmer. Right: A view of this courthouse being razed in 1956.

MEIGS COUNTY

Formed: January 20, 1836
Formed from: Hamilton, McMinn, and Rhea Counties
County seat: Decatur
Area: 195 sq.mi.

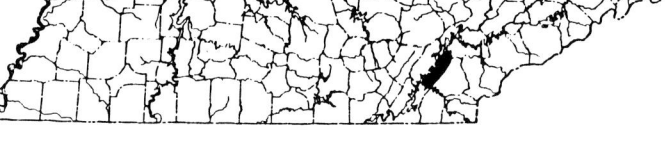

Meigs County was named for Return Jonathan Meigs, an officer in the Continental Army and the first state librarian. In 1801 he was appointed Indian agent for the Cherokee, where he remained until his death in 1823. The first court was organized at the home of James Stewart in 1836. The next court term was held at James Lillard's home, where a decision was made to erect a courthouse.[1]

The county seat, Decatur, was named in honor of Commodore Stephen Decatur. (The original county name was Vernon, after Senator Miles Vernon, and the county seat was Regan, after James Regan.[2])

The first courthouse was completed by William Kerr around 1839 for a cost of $2,400. It was a two story brick structure, 30 by 36 feet, and was occupied in December of 1837. The first floor had a single room with a brick floor while the second floor contained three rooms with a wood plank floor.[3]

This courthouse was replaced in 1882 by a two story brick structure. It featured a central, projecting, three story tower which had a convex-mansard roof.[4] This building was constructed for $4,000 and utilized brick made on the site.

Window and door lintels were trimmed with stone. This courthouse burned in 1902.

The current courthouse, Meigs County's third, was completed in 1904. This was also a two story brick structure, the design of which is very similar to the second courthouse. While it again features stone trimmed window lintels and an arched entry, the stocky brick tower does not project and has a low pyramidal roof with gables on each face.[5]

Left: The second Meigs County Courthouse, completed in 1882. Center: Ruins of the second courthouse after the 1902 fire. Right: The current courthouse during a 1904 Confederate Veteran reunion.

MONROE COUNTY

Formed: November 18, 1819
Formed from: From the Hiwassee Purchase
County seat: Madisonville
Area: 635 sq.mi.

Monroe County was named in honor of James Monroe, fifth President of the United States. The first court was organized in 1820 and held its first meetings at William Dickson's home on the Tennessee River.[1] The court continued to meet in various homes until a county seat was established at Tellico in 1825. Tellico's name was changed to Madisonville in 1830, in honor of President James Madison.[2]

The first courthouse was a log structure erected at Tellico. This burned in 1832 and was replaced sometime after 1835 by a brick structure. The second courthouse was used until it also burned in 1864, during the Civil War.[3] The courts then met in the basement of the old Tellico Lodge until a new courthouse could be built.

The third courthouse, completed in 1867, was a two story brick structure, 40 by 50 feet with two wings of two rooms each (each room was 18 feet square). John Minis proposed to do the carpentry and Denton and Peace were the contractors for the brickwork.[4] An 1868 newspaper account describes the structure as having a hipped roof, large windows with green shutters, four entries (one on each side with cross hallways) and was said to be very similar to the Loudon County Courthouse.[5] The interior had 12 fireplaces and two flights of stairs, one to each side of the main entrance. This courthouse was condemned in 1894, but the commissioners would not vote for a new courthouse at that time.

The current courthouse, Monroe County's fourth, was built in 1897 for approximately $17,000. This structure was praised at the time for being *substantial and well arranged on the interior* and having *no useless ornamentation on the outside*.[6]

The architects were the Bauman Brothers of Knoxville.[7] This two story brick structure sits on a high basement and features a tall central tower. Ornamentation consists of a stone watertable, a handsome cornice at the eave line of the hipped roofs and a one story entry porch with heavy square brick columns and a balustrade at the roof level. Similar square pilasters with Ionic and Doric capitals are used to frame the tower. An annex was added to the courthouse in 1979.

Left: Sketch of the 1867 courthouse by C.F. Hunt. Right: The current Monroe County Courthouse at its dedication.

MONTGOMERY COUNTY

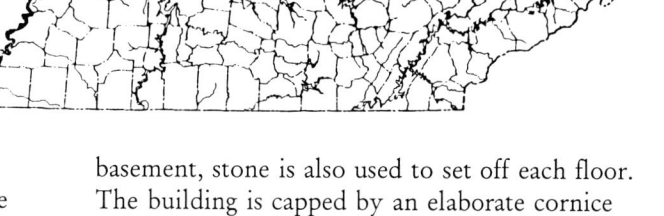

Formed: 1796
Formed from: Tennessee County
County seat: Clarksville
Area: 539 sq.mi.

Montgomery County was formed with Robertson County out of Tennessee County, a county created in 1788. It was named in honor of Colonel John Montgomery, who explored the Cumberland country in 1777. Clarksville, founded in 1784 and named for General George Rogers Clark, became the county seat. A log courthouse was ordered built around 1789. This structure, used until 1811, was built by James Adams on property adjoining his home on the public square.[1]

A new two story brick courthouse was built at the north end of the public square in 1811. It was 44 feet square and functioned until 1844. The lower floor consisted of one large room with an 18 foot ceiling, while the upper floor was divided into five rooms with 12 foot ceilings.[2] In 1844 a third courthouse was constructed on the north side of Franklin Street. This was destroyed by a fire in 1878.

A larger site was acquired for the fourth courthouse. Property was purchased on Commerce, bounded by Second and Third Streets and a new building was constructed in brick and stone in the monumental Second Empire style. The architect was George W. Bunting of Indianapolis. (Bunting was responsible for the design of numerous courthouses in Indiana as well as in Michigan, Kansas and West Virginia. Quite similar in form and style to the Montgomery County courthouse are courthouses in Indiana's Clinton and Johnson Counties.)

This courthouse cost $100,000 for the grounds, building, and furnishings. Sitting on a tall stone basement, stone is also used to set off each floor. The building is capped by an elaborate cornice and low hipped roof. A tall, square clock tower sits in the middle of the roof and tall pyramidal roofs are set at each corner. The courthouse was damaged by fire in 1900 and was restored to its original design. The building was renovated in 1966 and again in 1976.

Left: Opening of the fourth Montgomery County courthouse. Right: The current courthouse after the 1900 fire.

MOORE COUNTY

Formed: December 14, 1871
Formed from: Bedford, Coffee, Franklin, and Lincoln Counties
County seat: Lynchburg
Area: 129 sq.mi.

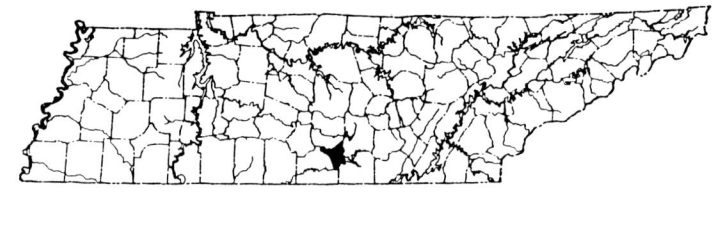

Moore County was named for Major General William Moore, a War of 1812 veteran, an early settler in Lincoln County and a member of the state House of Representatives. One of the smallest counties in the state, it was established in violation of the constitutional provision that each county have not less than 275 square miles. Lynchburg was selected as the county seat in 1872, but it was not until 1884 that a site was selected for the public square.

The courts were held in Tolley and Eaton's Hall (the Old Red Hall) until a courthouse was completed in 1885. Still in use, this is a substantial two story brick structure originally constructed for $6,875. It is 40 by 60 feet and the original plan had offices on the first floor and the courtroom on the second.[1] The exterior of the courthouse is elaborately decorated with arched door and window lintels and an elaborate cornice. In the middle of the low hip roof is an equally elegant square cupola surmounted by a finial.

This courthouse was renovated in 1968. At that time it was enlarged with two story wings to either side. The exterior detailing of the wings carefully matched the design and detailing of the original courthouse.

A view of the courthouse c1955, prior to the addition of two story wings to either side.

MORGAN COUNTY

Formed: October 15, 1817
Formed from: Roane County
County seat: Wartburg
Area: 522 sq.mi.

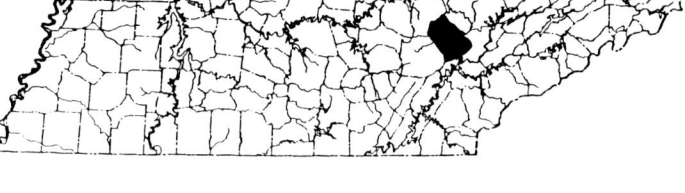

Morgan County was named in honor of Brigadier General Daniel Morgan, a veteran of the French and Indian War who also served under Benedict Arnold during the Revolutionary War. The original county seat was Montgomery, in honor of Major Lemuel P. Montgomery. The first court convened in at the Indian Tavern until the log courthouse was ready.

With the creation of Fentress County in 1823, partly out of Morgan, Montgomery was no longer the geographical center. A new county seat was established in 1825 with the same name, about one mile west of Wartburg. A temporary courthouse was constructed on the square and a permanent courthouse was proposed, but this was never constructed.

As German settlers were recruited, a new town of Wartburg was platted in 1845. This colony was still struggling to survive in 1850, having had its offer to build a courthouse and jail on the public square rejected if the county seat moved. A courthouse was apparently constructed to a design by Fredrick B. Guenther, using private funds to entice this county seat relocation.[1]

The county seat was finally moved to Wartburg in 1870. A two story frame courthouse on a stone foundation was completed the following year. Built for $3,132 by A.J. Hurtt and Johann Kreis, this structure had a recessed two story entry porch and, in addition to the courtroom, it had a jury room and four rooms for county offices.

This courthouse was replaced by Morgan County's current, fourth courthouse in 1904. It is a two story brick building with projecting corner pavilions. The pavilions have pyramidal roofs and the courthouse itself a hip roof with a tall square clock tower in the center. It was designed by W. Chamberlin and Co., Architects. W.R. Harper was the contractor who completed the building at a cost of $18,000. A private electric power system was used to light the courthouse in 1924.[2]

Left: The frame courthouse constructed in 1871. Right: An early 20th century view of the current courthouse.

OBION COUNTY

Formed: October 24, 1823
Formed from: The Western District
County seat: Union City
Area: 545 sq.mi.

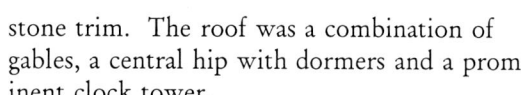

Obion County was named for the Obion River, the chief watercourse of the county. The county seat was originally established in Troy in 1823. The first court was held at the home of William Wilson in 1824. A shift in population and power relating to the building of the railroad resulted in the county seat moving to Union City in 1890.

However, three courthouses were constructed at Troy. The first was an 18 by 20 log structure with one door and one window.[1] It was built on the public square in 1825. This was replaced by a fifty foot square two story brick courthouse in 1831. The second courthouse was partially destroyed by an earthquake in 1842. It was taken down and rebuilt using the same materials.[2]

In 1852 a third courthouse was built. This was a simple two story frame structure with a low hip roof and chimneys at each corner.[3] Entrances were located on at least two of the four elevations. The building was used as a stable by Federal troops during the Civil War. It was later converted into a school after the county seat moved to Union City.[4]

The fourth courthouse, the first at Union City, was built in 1890. It was a two story brick structure set on a stone foundation and utilizing stone trim. The roof was a combination of gables, a central hip with dormers and a prominent clock tower.

The present (fifth) courthouse was built in 1939 for $200,000, with partial funding by the Public Works Administration. This is a three story structure (including the basement), 75 by 100 feet. Marr and Holman of Nashville were the architects. The design of this structure is the streamlined classical design favored during this period.

Left: The third courthouse at Troy. Center: The architect's drawing for the 1890 courthouse. Left: Obion County's fourth (1890) courthouse, the first at Union City.

OVERTON COUNTY

Formed: September 11, 1806
Formed from: Jackson County
County seat: Livingston
Area: 433 sq.mi.

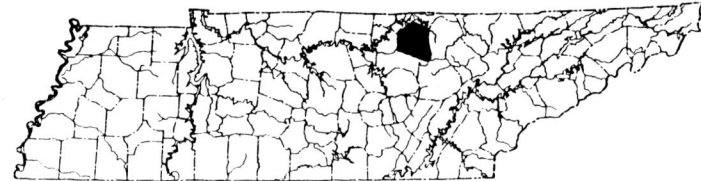

Overton County was named in honor of John Overton, a pioneer attorney and judge of the state Supreme Court. He was also the co-founder of Memphis. The first court was held at Jones Store, five miles north of Livingston. Monroe was the first county seat, where a log courthouse was constructed in 1808. The county seat was moved to Livingston in 1835 (named for Edgar Livingston, Secretary of State in President Jackson's cabinet).

Three courthouses have been constructed in Livingston, the first in 1835 in the center of the public square. This was a three room brick structure consisting of a courtroom and two offices. The next courthouse, built in 1855, was a two story brick structure. It was destroyed by fire in 1865.[1]

The county's present courthouse, its third, was built in 1869. This is a two story brick structure, built by Josiah S. Copeland for $9,999.99.[2] It was constructed on the foundations of the old courthouse and its description is completely noted in the minutes of the October Term Court of 1868.[3] Rectangular in plan, the courthouse is simply detailed and has a gable roof with pediment detailing at each end. It originally had four 17 by 20 foot rooms on the first floor, one in each corner and all separated by a cross-shaped hallway. The courthouse had doors on all four sides into these hallways. Two stairways lead to the second floor, which consisted of a courtroom and two jury rooms (along the west side).

The courthouse underwent major repairs in 1934, during which time vaults were added, and again in 1957. The Bohannon Building, an annex to the courthouse, was completed in 1936. It was built in stone using WPA labor for a cost of $15,000.[4] In 1978-79 the interior of the courthouse was renovated.

An early, undated view of the present Overton County Courthouse.

PERRY COUNTY

Formed: November 18, 1819
Formed from: Hickman County
County seat: Linden
Area: 415 sq.mi.

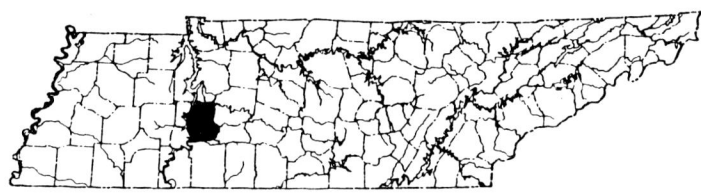

Perry County was named in honor of Commodore Oliver Hazard Perry. The county originally embraced the territory of both Perry and Decatur counties, the latter being split off in 1846. The county seat was first established at Perryville in 1821, where it remained until 1846 when it was moved to Harrisburg following the formation of Decatur County. By six votes, the county seat was moved in 1848 to Linden.

At Perryville the first court was held at the home of James Dickson.[1] Two courthouses were also constructed there, the first of logs, and a second in brick.[2] At Linden, the first courthouse was also constructed of logs in 1848. This functioned until 1849 when a frame courthouse was built. The frame courthouse was consumed by fire during the Civil War, along with many county records.

A fifth courthouse was completed in 1868. This was a two story brick structure with a gable roof. The principal elevation had a pedimented recessed two story entrance portico. Costing $9,500, it had offices on the first floor and the courtroom on the second. This building accidentally burned in 1928, during its renovation.

The present courthouse, Perry County's sixth, was completed in 1928 at a cost of $47,000. It is a classically-inspired three story structure with a full basement. The exterior is finished in brick and stone, with an elaborately detailed entrance in stone. On the top two floors stone quoins are used at the corners on the walls as paired pilasters to form a two story giant order topped by a full entablature.

Perry County's 1868 courthouse.

PICKETT COUNTY

Formed: February 25, 1879
Formed from: Fentress and Overton Counties
County seat: Byrdstown
Area: 163 sq.mi.

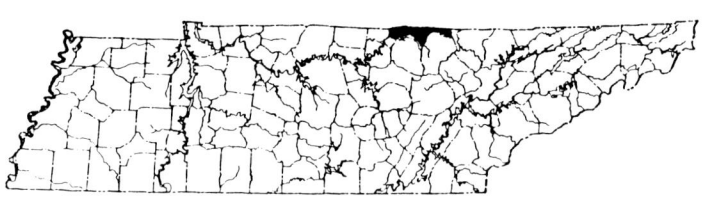

Pickett County, formed from portions of Fentress and Overton Counties, was the last county formed in Tennessee. It was named for Howell L. Pickett, a state representative from Wilson County. The first session of the county court was held in Smyrna in 1881. The first session of the circuit court met in a church in Smyrna.[1] After several sessions, it was voted to move the county seat to Byrdstown. Byrdstown was named for Senator Byrd, and was located on land originally owned by John Sevier.

The first courthouse was completed in 1881 and was a two story brick structure on a 24-inch thick limestone foundation.[2] It appears to have been basically square in plan and somewhat eclectic in style. Low segmental arched windows contrast with pointed Gothic-style windows in the stairway. The courthouse was topped with a cupola in the middle of its low hipped roof. The cupola roof was unusual in that it incorporated wall dormer windows on each side. The bid of $5,500 submitted by Babbs & Grimes for the construction of this courthouse was approved by the court.[3] In 1934 the courthouse burned together with all its records.

The current courthouse, completed in 1935, was designed by Marr and Holman of Nashville, with Niles Yearwood as the contractor. The three story building was constructed with concrete floors and walls, with clay tile interior walls.[4] The exterior is faced with crab orchard stone quarried locally.[5] Inmates from the jail were used to help construct this building.

Left: Pickett County's first courthouse (1881). Right: The current courthouse under construction.

POLK COUNTY

Formed: November 28, 1839
Formed from: Bradley and McMinn Counties
County seat: Benton
Area: 435 sq.mi.

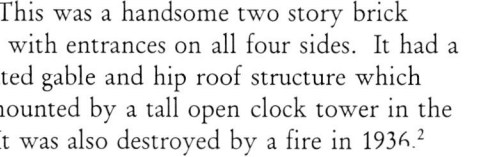

Polk County was named for James Knox Polk, then governor of Tennessee and later the 11th President of the United States. The county seat, Benton, was named for Thomas Hart Benton, a U.S. Senator for 30 years.

The first courthouse was completed in 1840 and was of frame construction, 30 by 20 feet. The June Term (1840) court records describe it as being a one story (10 foot) high structure covered with ...*three Ft. Boards. Built of good scantlling well weather Boarded up. 2 plain doors and two windows a good floor of 1 inch plank well jointed and nailed down.* It was located on the public square just north of the current courthouse.[1]

A second courthouse, completed in 1848, was a two brick structure. Court Term minutes outline the specifications for this structure, which was to be 45 feet square and have walls 27 feet high. The courtroom was on the first floor, which was finished with brick and had three entry doors. Stairways were to be located in either corner flanking the judge's bench. The second floor had an eight foot wide corridor with two rooms to one side and one on the other side. The front of this courthouse faced northwest. This structure burned in 1895.

The third courthouse was completed in 1897 for $9,000. This was a handsome two story brick structure with entrances on all four sides. It had a complicated gable and hip roof structure which was surmounted by a tall open clock tower in the center. It was also destroyed by a fire in 1936.[2]

The present courthouse, Polk County's fourth, was designed by Reuben H. Hunt. It was completed in 1937 by Forcum Jones Company, contractor. It was completed at a cost of $100,000, which was partially funded by the Federal Emergency Administration of Public Works.[3]

Unusual to Polk County is a second courthouse in Ducktown, because the county is divided by the Ocoee River and Chilhowie Mountains. The old courthouse in Ducktown was a simple two story wood frame structure with a corner tower. This structure burned in 1947.[4] The current court facilities are incorporated in a one story brick multi-use structure.

Left: Polk County's 1897 courthouse. Right: The old Ducktown courthouse.

PUTNAM COUNTY

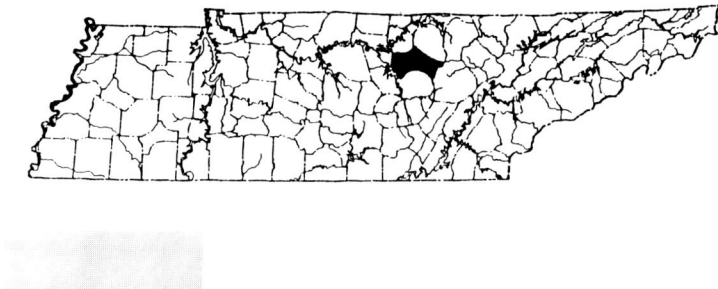

Formed: February 11, 1854
Formed from: DeKalb, Jackson, Overton, and White Counties
County seat: Cookeville
Area: 401 sq.mi.

Putnam County was named in honor of Israel Putnam, a veteran of the French and Indian War and Revolutionary War general. Elected courts were established and functioning until 1844, when an injunction forced the re-establishment of the county. This occurred in 1854 through the efforts of Maj. Cooke, for whom the county seat of Cookeville was named.

The first courthouse, built in 1856, was burned during the Civil War. A second courthouse, completed in 1866, burned in 1898 with a substantial loss of county records.

The present courthouse was completed in 1900 at a cost of $30,000. It was designed by James H. Yeaman, and Scott and Smoot were the contractors. This is a three story brick structure with three octagonal projecting corner pavilions. The fourth corner, square in plan, terminated in a tall, domed clock tower.

The courthouse was remodelled in 1962. Wilson and Odom were the architects for that renovation.[1] The exterior of the courthouse has been heavily altered through the removal of its original roof, clock tower and Flemish gable wall dormers.

A view of the current Putnam County courthouse in 1912.

RHEA COUNTY

Formed: November 30, 1807
Formed from: Roane County
County seat: Dayton
Area: 316 sq.mi.

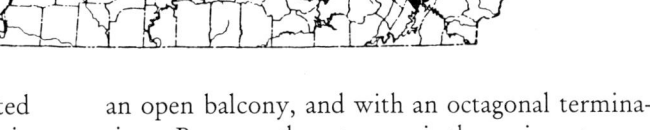

Rhea County was named for John Rhea, Revolutionary War veteran, member of the 1796 Tennessee Constitutional Convention, member of the state and later U.S. House of Representatives, and an early leader in higher education. The first court was held at the Big Springs home of William Henry in 1808 and continued there until 1812, when Washington was established as the county seat.[1]

Two courthouses were built at Washington. The first, completed in 1813, was a two story frame structure, thirty feet square. It was built on the public square by James Mitchell for $936.25. A second, brick courthouse was completed in 1831 by Thomas Crutchfield (a contractor who erected similar buildings for no less than eight counties in East Tennessee).[2] This building was partially destroyed by a tornado in 1833.

The county seat was moved to Dayton in 1890, after the railroad from Cincinnati to Chattanooga was completed through it. The present courthouse was completed in 1891. It was designed by W. Chamberlin and Company of Knoxville and Dowling and Taylor were the contractors. The Dayton courthouse is a three story brick structure. The principal facade combines a low, three story pyramidal roofed corner tower offset on the opposite corner by a tall, square clock tower with an open balcony, and with an octagonal termination. Between these towers is the main entrance under a one story porch.

It was this courthouse that provided the scene for the now famous Scopes evolution ("Monkey") trial held in 1925. The trial pitted William Jennings Bryan and Clarence Darrow in a legal battle that won national attention through the first national radio hook-up.[3]

Left: The current Rhea County Courthouse prior to its 1976 restoration. Right: A view of the observers benches set up under the trees on the courthouse lawn for the Scopes trial.

ROANE COUNTY

Formed: December 20, 1801
Formed from: Blount and Knox Counties
County seat: Kingston
Area: 361 sq.mi.

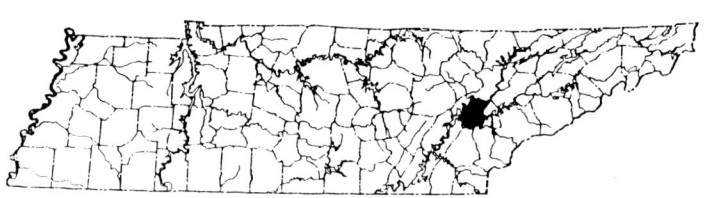

Roane County was named for Archibald Roane, member of the 1796 Constitutional Convention and second governor of Tennessee. The county seat was set at Kingston (which was established in 1799) and was named for Robert King, an early settler who owned the land on which the town was built.[1] Kingston served as capital of Tennessee for one day when the Legislature met there on September 21, 1807. The first Court of Pleas and Quarter Sessions was organized in December 1801 at the home of Hugh Beatty.[2]

The first courthouse, a brick structure completed around 1814 (1803 according to Goodspeed), had a handsome cupola or dome.[3] The second courthouse, completed in 1856, still stands but is no longer in use as such. This Greek Revival structure was designed by Frederick B. Guenther.[4] It was built by John Lowery and Augustus Fisher for $9,400. The structure has been described as
...among the most commodious and splendid buildings of the kind in the state... and features an unusual split-level floor plan design.[5] Basically a two story building, three floors of offices are located in the two front corners flanking the main recessed entry portico. On that elevation there are three levels of windows, while on the adjoining side elevations only two.

Turn-of-the-century renovations included the addition of the north porch and attic dormers. During the middle 1930s, an east wing was constructed as part of a Public Works Administration project. In the early 1970s a move was made to demolish the old courthouse and to build a new one. The Roane County Heritage Commission was established to save this historic courthouse, receiving the deed to the structure in 1975.

Roane County's current courthouse was completed in 1975 at a cost of $1,200,000. It was designed by architect Martin J. Lide and was constructed by Webb Construction of Athens. The classically-inspired design features a center projecting pedimented portico flanked by smaller wings with similar porticoes.

Left: The second courthouse in the late 19th century. Right: A pre-1930s postcard view showing the second courthouse without its WPA addition.

ROBERTSON COUNTY

Formed: April 9, 1796
Formed from: Tennessee County
County seat: Springfield
Area: 476 sq.mi.

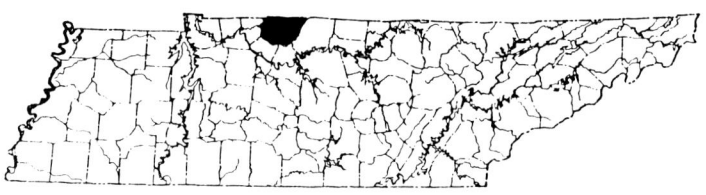

Robertson County was named in honor of James Robertson, leader in the establishment of the Watauga settlement, and also leader of the expedition in 1779 to found Nashborough (Nashville). Robertson and Montgomery Counties were formed together from the old Tennessee County at the time of statehood. The county was organized at the home of Jacob McCarty on Sulphur Fork, west of Springfield. Springfield, founded in 1788, became established as the county seat and finally incorporating in 1853.

The first courthouse was completed in 1799. This was an 18 by 18 foot log building covered with clapboard.[1] It was located on the public square and was sold in 1819 for $116.55. This was followed by a second structure, considered very "modern" and completed on the same site for $6,598. It was a two story brick building 40 by 40 feet and had its courtroom on the first floor, while offices for the sheriff and clerk of the court were on the second. This courthouse was pronounced unsafe and dangerous in 1879.[2]

The current courthouse, Robertson County's third, was completed in 1881 for $20,959.40 by Patton and McInturff, contractors. It was designed by architect William C. Smith. The original design consisted of a two story buff-colored brick structure with stone trim. It had an asymmetrical roof configuration consisting of a large convex mansard pavilion at one corner and a smaller tall and square straight mansard roof in an opposite corner. Both towers and the low main roof ridge line were capped with elegant cast iron cresting. The tall, arched windows still retain their elegant sheet metal hood moldings. The current structure was renovated in 1930 by architects Dougherty & Gardner of Nashville.[3] The Second Empire components were removed, a central clock tower and north and south wings were added and the entire elevation was converted to a completely symmetrical design.

Two postcard views of the current Robertson County courthouse. Left: The current courthouse prior to its 1930 renovation. Right: The 1930 renovation design.

RUTHERFORD COUNTY

Formed: October 25, 1803
Formed from: Davidson County
County seat: Murfreesboro
Area: 619 sq.mi.

Rutherford County was named for Major General Griffith Rutherford, a member of the Revolutionary Army. Jefferson (named for Thomas Jefferson) was selected as the first county seat in 1805. Here, a brick courthouse was erected in the center of the public square.[1] In 1811, the county seat was moved to Cannonsburg (after Governor Newton Cannon of Williamson County). In 1817 the name was changed to Murfreesborough, and later Murfreesboro (for Colonel Hardy Murfree).

The first courthouse at Cannonsburg/Murfreesboro was completed in 1813. This structure was renovated in 1817 and, beginning in 1819, served as the state capitol building until 1822, when it burned.[2] The next courthouse was completed in 1822 and functioned until 1859. It was of brick construction and cost $6,000.[3]

Rutherford County's current courthouse, its fourth, was completed in 1859 with James H. Yeaman as supervising architect, at a cost of $50,000. This was a two story brick structure with a low hip roof and tall clock tower. Projecting porticoes (with evenly spaced columns) were found on the east and west elevations, while smaller entries were provided to the north and south. In 1861, additions and improvements were made, including a privy house, carpet for the circuit courtroom floor, and brick paving around the courthouse.[4]

Following the Civil War additional repairs and additions were completed.

Over the years numerous exterior and interior improvements to the courthouse have been documented.[5] Substantial improvements were undertaken in 1906. The work completed by 1908 included the addition of a third floor.

The present cupola was added and the paired column arrangement on the east and west facades occurred sometime prior to 1912. In 1913 the courthouse was damaged by high winds during a tornado. In 1924 the columns around the cupola were replaced. The last major alteration to the courthouse consisted of the addition of north and south wings, added in 1965.

Left: The current courthouse with its evenly spaced columns and original cupola design in the late 19th century. Right: The current courthouse following the addition of the third floor, pairing of portico columns and changed cupola design.

SCOTT COUNTY

Formed: December 17, 1849
Formed from: Anderson, Fentress, and Morgan Counties
County seat: Huntsville
Area: 532 sq.mi.

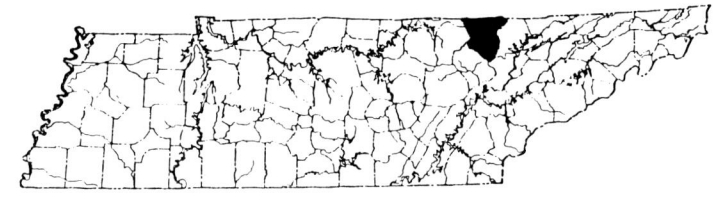

Scott County was named for General Winfield Scott, commanding general in the Mexican War. Huntsville, the county seat, was laid out in 1850 and was supposedly named in honor of early hunters.

The first courthouse was completed in 1851. It was a two story frame clapboard clad structure with a gable roof that was used until 1874. The second courthouse, smaller than the first, was built of brick, was two stories high and also had a low gable roof. It remained in use until it was replaced in 1906.[1]

The third courthouse, completed in 1906, was constructed of local sandstone. It featured four corner pavilions with pyramidal roofs and a central clock tower on its hip roof. The contractor was Ruth Holmes. This structure was destroyed by fire in 1946, leaving only the stone walls standing.[2]

The current courthouse consists of a two story brick-clad structure built around the shell of the third courthouse at a cost of $225,000. It was completed in 1948. One story wings were added to either side of the shell. Clem H. Myer was the architect and John H. Johnson & Sons was the contractor.

Left: A view of the first courthouse c1870. Center: Scott County's second courthouse c1905. Top Right: The third courthouse completed in 1906. Bottom Right: The current courthouse prior to the gable roof addition.

SEQUATCHIE COUNTY

Formed: December 9, 1857
Formed from: Bledsoe and Hamilton Counties
County seat: Dunlap
Area: 266 sq.mi.

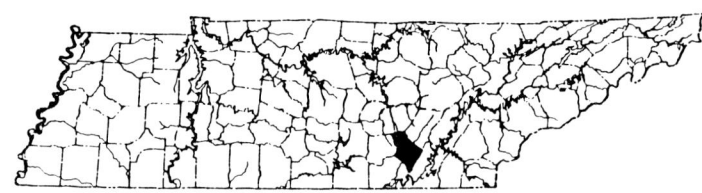

Sequatchie County was named for the valley in which the county lies, which had been named for a Cherokee chief. The first court met at the home of Joel Wheeler in Fillmore (Walnut Valley). In 1858 the county seat was centrally located at Coop's Creek, and the name was soon changed to Dunlap.[1]

The first courthouse was a simple, basically square, two story frame structure. Very plain in design, this courthouse had a single entrance under a one story porch and was topped by a low hipped roof with a widow's walk. A front gable was located over the entrance.

The present courthouse was built in 1911 at a cost of $12,000. It was built by W. K. Brown and Brothers and is in a Colonial Revival style. A two story brick structure, it has a two story projecting portico. The principal elevation has been enriched by two story brick pilasters and the structure is covered by a hipped roof.

Left: The first Sequatchie County courthouse. Right: The current courthouse under construction.

SEVIER COUNTY

Formed: September 27, 1794
Formed from: Jefferson County
County seat: Sevierville
Area: 592 sq.mi.

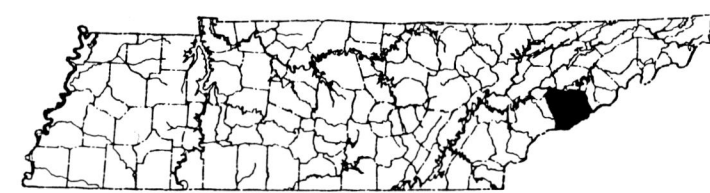

Sevier County was named in honor of John Sevier, a colonel in the Revolutionary Army, governor of the State of Franklin, and first governor of Tennessee. The State of Franklin, organized in 1784, created three counties in 1785, one of which was Sevier. The first county courts were held at Newell's Station.[1] The State of Franklin was dissolved in 1788 and it was not until 1794 that Sevier County was formalized by the Territorial Legislature.

The first court met at the house of Isaac Thomas. Tradition has it, however, that the first courts were held in a stable said to be so infested with fleas that the lawyers had it burned.[2] Sevierville, the county seat, was also established and named in 1795. The town was laid out in that year on 25 acres of land purchased from James McMahan.[3] Around 1796, the first courthouse was constructed of logs. This was followed by a frame structure in 1820. The third courthouse, of brick, was completed in 1850 and burned in 1856 together with all its contents.[4]

A new site, one acre at the junction of Main and Cross Streets, was selected for the fourth courthouse, which was completed in 1856. This has since become the town square. Constructed was a two story brick structure with a wide two story columned and pedimented portico. A circular cupola was located in the center of the hip roof. This courthouse was used until 1895.[5]

Plans for the fifth and current courthouse included the purchase of a new tract of land. The structure was designed by McDonald Brothers, Architects of Louisville. It was completed in 1896 at a cost of $21,000 by C. W. Brown, of Lenoir City. The courthouse is an imposing two story brick structure 85 by 70 feet, with a 130-foot central tower.[6] The building sits on a stone base and has projecting pavilions with domed cupolas at each corner, a triple arched principal entrance and an arcade at the second floor above the entrance.

The architectural significance of this building was recognized in 1971 when it became the first courthouse in Tennessee to be listed on the National Register of Historic Places. The nomination stated that ...*it is very significant that such an example of Beaux-Arts Classicism architecture should be found in a rural county*....[7] In 1971 a complete renovation of the building and grounds began and included an annex. The designer was Community Tectonics of Gatlinburg. The contractor was Carol Cates & Sons of Clinton, with the final cost of the renovation being $1,375,000.

Top: The current courthouse at the turn-of-the-century.
Bottom: The fourth Sevier County Courthouse(1856).

SHELBY COUNTY

Formed: November 24, 1819
Formed from: Hardin County
County seat: Memphis
Area: 755 sq.mi.

Shelby County was named for Isaac Shelby, appointed with Andrew Jackson as U.S. Commissioner and with whom he arranged the purchase of the Western District from the Chickasaw Indian Nation in 1818. Memphis, twice the county seat, was named by General James Winchester because of supposed references to the city in ancient Egypt.[1]

Memphis' streets were laid out in 1819 with market and court squares. In 1821 $175 was set aside to erect a temporary log courthouse said to be *...wanting in capacity or comfort or both as the courts frequently met at private houses.*[2] Thomas D. Carr was the builder[3] of this courthouse, which was built at the market square as the other was too far out. A second temporary courthouse was constructed in this location and became a meeting house when the county courts relocated from Memphis to Raleigh.[4]

Sanderlin's Bluff was acquired in 1827 for a new county seat and was named Raleigh. $550 was allocated to complete public buildings and a small frame courthouse was built there by Joseph Coe.[5] This was replaced in 1834 by a brick structure, 40 by 50 feet, and two stories high. This courthouse functioned until the county seat moved back to Memphis in 1866.[6]

In Memphis, a lot was acquired and a $150,000 loan obtained in 1861 for a new courthouse. However, construction was delayed by the Civil War. In 1874 the Overton Hotel was purchased and repaired for $150,000. The county courts moved into this, followed by the federal courts and court officers in 1875.

The current Shelby County Courthouse was completed in 1909. It was designed by New York architect James Gamble Rogers. This neo-Classical Ionic order structure was constructed of Bedford limestone at a cost of $1,500,000. The interior marble work comes from Tennessee, Alabama, Vermont, and Pennsylvania. John Gaisford of Memphis was the supervising architect for this project.[7]

Left: The Overton Hotel, site of the 1874 courthouse.
Right: An early view of the current Shelby County Courthouse.

SMITH COUNTY

Formed: October 26, 1799
Formed from: Sumner County
County seat: Carthage
Area: 314 sq.mi.

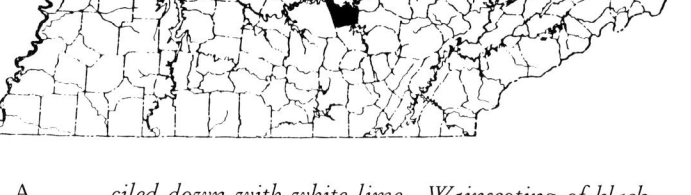

Smith County was named for Daniel Smith, colonel in the Revolutionary Army, surveyor, and cartographer of the first map of Tennessee. The first court was held in the home of Tilman Dixon at Dixon Springs. In 1801 an act called for the establishment of a county seat called Smithfield, but no action was taken.[1] In 1803 a county seat was established at Livingston, where 40 acres had been purchased and a town laid out. Construction was also begun on a courthouse, but this was abandoned in 1803 even though the materials had already been purchased and delivered.[2]

The courts continued to be held in residences until Carthage (formerly Walton's Ferry) was selected as the county seat in 1804. The first courthouse was erected in 1805.[3] This structure was brick, 50 feet square and two stories high. A square cupola was located in the center of its hip roof. It contained four offices and a hall on the first floor and two offices and a courtroom on the second. All of the rooms had large wood fireplaces. It was used until 1879.[4]

The current courthouse was completed in 1877. Costing $18,000, this was a two story brick structure in the Second Empire style. It was built by contractor Henry C. Jackson of Murfreesboro to plans and specifications provided by E.P. Turner of Carthage.[5] T.J. Shelton of Lebanon completed the stonework.[6] This structure was described at the time as follows: *The walls were built of good hard brick and, after completion, were cleaned and washed off with apple vinegar and penciled down with white lime. Wainscoting of black walnut and yellow pine three feet in height was put up around all rooms, including the courtroom. Stair rails and banisters were of three inch fancy turned black walnut. The mansard roof was covered with Vermont slate of purple and green color.*[7]

The older courthouse was finally demolished in 1879, following the opening of the new structure. When first built, the current courthouse was somewhat different than today, having two front doors and two sets of stairs instead of one.[8] It was renovated in the 1970s at a cost of $200,000.

Left: A modern view of "Dixona," the home of Tilman Dixon and site of the early county courts. Right: An early 20th century view of Smith County's current courthouse.

STEWART COUNTY

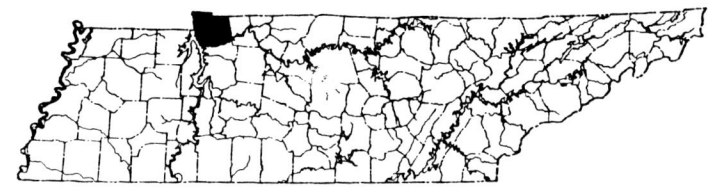

Formed: November 1, 1803
Formed from: Montgomery County
County seat: Dover
Area: 458 sq.mi.

Stewart County was named in honor of Duncan Stewart, a Revolutionary War veteran and early settler in the area. Dover (originally intended to be called Monroe) was established as the county seat in 1805. The first county court was held at the home of William Martin. Thirty acres of land was purchased from Robert Nelson for the new county seat and a one story double log courthouse was completed in 1806 for $600.[1]

A commission was established to look into a new courthouse in 1816, but the results of the commission are not known. The second courthouse was planned by the next commission and was completed in 1823. This cost $8,000, was brick, 40 feet square, and two stories in height. It was destroyed by the Union army in 1862. However, by prior agreement between the county officials and the Union forces, all of the county records were removed for safe-keeping.[2]

The county's third courthouse was completed in 1870 for $14,000. It was also constructed of brick, was square in plan and two stories tall, and had a tin roof with a cupola. Josh Whitney was the mason for the construction of the building. Offices were located on the first floor and the courtroom on the second.[3] Two annexes were later been added to the courthouse. This structure was torn down in 1965.

The current courthouse, Stewart County's fourth, was completed in 1965 on a site adjoining the public square. The architects were Wilson and Odom.

A view of the 1870 courthouse taken prior to its demolition in 1965.

SULLIVAN COUNTY

Formed: 1779
Formed from: Washington County
County seat: Blountville
Area: 413 sq.mi.

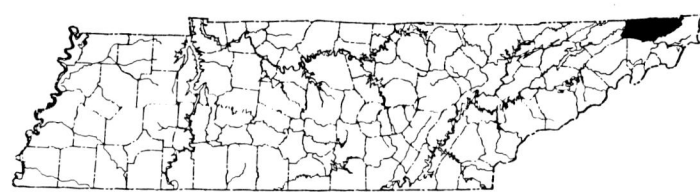

Sullivan County was named for Major General John Sullivan, officer in the Revolutionary War, member of the Continental Congress and president of New Hampshire. This county was created by North Carolina and was the second county formed in Tennessee. The county court was organized at the home of Moses Looney in February 1780. For a few years the courts were held at the Lancy Tavern near Eaton's Station or at the house of Mrs. Sharp near the mouth of Muddy Creek.[1]

With the erection of Hawkins County in 1786 there was a need to find a more central location of the seat of justice. Until the selection of a county seat, the courts met at the home of Joseph Cole. In 1792 James Brigham donated the land on which the permanent county seat was laid out.[2] Blountville, named for Governor William Blount, was thus established and a courthouse of massive hewn logs was completed there in 1795.

The log courthouse functioned for nearly 30 years, until the completion of a new courthouse built of hand-fired brick in 1825. John Dameron, builder of the 1835 Hawkins County courthouse, may have been the builder of this structure.[3] A wing was added in 1850. This courthouse was replaced in 1853 by a new structure was that gutted by a fire, together with most its records, during the Civil War in 1863. While the interior and the roof burned, the walls remained intact and this structure was rebuilt in 1866 by contractors James Hunt and John Lyle.[4]

The current courthouse exterior dates from an extensive 1920 renovation. The Classical Revival style design features a handsome two story pedimented Ionic portico. A new jail was added to the rear in 1956. The 1866 cupola was removed in the 1970s. The interior features a wide marble stairway in the great entrance to a circular balcony. On the second floor is a large panelled courtroom.[5]

Two views of the 1866 courthouse.

SUMNER COUNTY

Formed: November 17, 1786
Formed from: Davidson County
County seat: Gallatin
Area: 529 sq.mi.

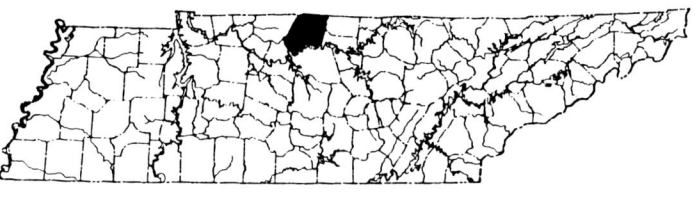

Sumner County was named in honor of Major General Jethro Sumner, an officer in the French and Indian War and was created by an act of the North Carolina legislature. The county seat, Gallatin, was named for Albert Gallatin, Thomas Jefferson's Secretary of the Treasury. The early courts moved from residence to residence. In 1790 a small log building was erected at West Station Camp Creek. This was used until 1793, when the courts went back to residences until Gallatin was established in 1801.

The first courthouse was completed in 1803. It had a courtroom on the first floor and offices on the second. Used until 1837, when it was replaced by a more commodious structure, it was a nearly square two story brick structure. The simple Greek Revival detailing featured corner pilasters as well as recessed entries on two elevations. The metal hip roof was surmounted by an octagonal cupola, which was replaced with a square cupola during renovations in 1867. In this structure the county court and four offices were located on the first floor, while the circuit/chancery court rooms and two offices were found on the second.[1]

The current courthouse, Sumner County's third, was completed in 1940. It was designed by Nashville architects Marr and Holman. This courthouse cost $170,000 and was partially funded by a federal grant. The design is an example of Marr and Holman's severely restrained classical design style.

Left: An early illustration of the second courthouse prior to the 1867 renovations. Center: A late 19th century view of the second courthouse with an altered cupola design. Right: A c1950 view of the current Sumner County courthouse.

TIPTON COUNTY

Formed: October 29, 1823
Formed from: The Western District
County seat: Covington
Area: 459 sq.mi.

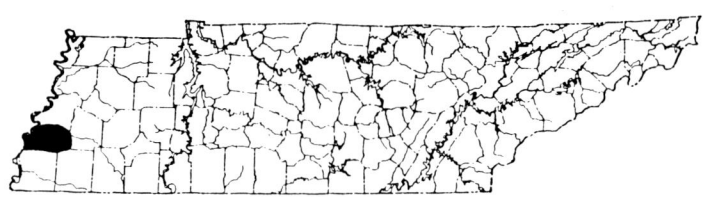

Tipton County was named for Captain Jacob Tipton, who raised a company for the defense of the Northwest Territory against the Indians and was killed leading an attack. A sum of $350 was allocated for a courthouse in 1825 and a frame structure was completed at the northeast corner of the public square later that year. The center of the square was left vacant for a permanent brick courthouse to be erected at a later date.[1]

In 1830 funds were appropriated for a new two story brick courthouse which was built by Carr Cox and William Walton. This Greek Revival style structure was occupied in 1832. It had a pedimented portico and a center octagonal cupola. By 1889 this courthouse was in poor condition, having been extensively repaired in 1875 after a "terrific" storm where ...*the roof of the courthouse was plainly distinguished as it came sailing over like an inverted cone.*[2] This courthouse was abandoned in 1889 and was subsequently torn down.

The present courthouse, the county's third, was completed in 1890 at a cost of $24,500. It was designed by McDonald Brothers, architects and built by W.F. Boone. As with the second courthouse, this structure occupies the center of the public square. An early description of this courthouse still survives: *The hall, which was the last part of the building finished, is spanned by two beautiful arches. The main entrance is on the north, which is adorned by a porch and stone steps. The stairway to the courtroom is situated in the south end, which prevents the hall from showing to so good an advantage as it does from the north. The floor of the hall is made of Tennessee marble, the walls plastered and nicely finished. These walls are yet unadorned by the hands of the vandal scribbler....*

The offices are located as follows: Entering the building from the north, the first on the left ground floor is the chairman's office; second, county clerk's; third, registrar's office; and the fourth, the sheriff's office. There are two rooms at the landing of the stairs on the second floor...one of these will be used for a grand jury room and the other for a witness room. There are also two rooms on the same floor for the use of the petit jury and a consultation room just behind the judge's stand.[3]

In 1909 a tornado damaged the courthouse tower. By 1928 a decision had been made to remove the tower and repair the roof, as the tower remained in dangerous structural condition.

Left: The second Tipton County Courthouse (1832). Right: The 1909 tornado damage to the current courthouse.

TROUSDALE COUNTY

Formed: June 21, 1870
Formed from: Macon, Smith, Sumner, and Wilson Counties
County seat: Hartsville
Area: 114 sq.mi.

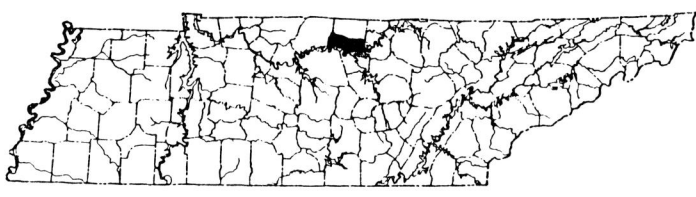

Trousdale County was named in honor of William Trousdale, who served with Andrew Jackson at Pensacola and New Orleans, was governor of Tennessee, and later served as U.S. minister to Brazil. The county seat, Hartsville, was named for James Hart, whose land was purchased for the town. The first court was held in the Hartsville Methodist Church.

The county's first courthouse was completed in 1875 by Joe Patton at a cost of $10,082.15. It burned in 1900 and was replaced 1901, only to burn again in 1904.[1] The third courthouse, completed in December of 1904 also burned, together with all the records.[2]

The current courthouse, a three story brick structure on a stone foundation, was completed in 1906. It features a handsome entry porch, decorative stepped gables, and a small cupola in the center of its hip roof. Decorative brick bands enliven the masonry walls at each floor level. Modern one story brick additions have been added to either side of the courthouse.

Left: The current Trousdale County Courthouse shortly after its completion. Right: The courthouse during the great flood.

UNICOI COUNTY

Formed: March 19, 1875
Formed from: Carter and Washington Counties
County seat: Erwin
Area: 186 sq.mi.

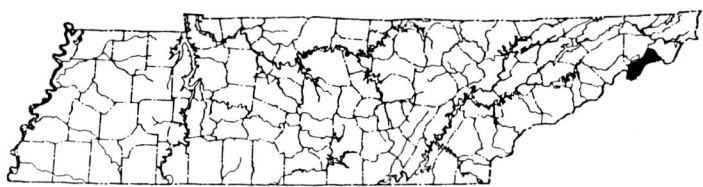

Unicoi County was named for an Indian tribal name, Unaka, meaning "white." This was also the name given to the mountain range in the county. The county seat was first named Vanderbilt in hopes of attracting Cornelius Vanderbilt to the area. In 1879 the name was changed to Ervin in honor of D.J. N Ervin, an outstanding local citizen. Eventually the name was changed to Erwin to honor the county's first court clerk, Jesse B. Erwin.[1]

The first court met in January 1876 at the Indian Creek Baptist Church. The first courthouse, a two story brick structure, was completed in 1876. This building was a very simple rectangular structure with a low hipped roof, in the center of which was a square cupola.

In 1915, this courthouse was replaced by a two story brick structure. It also had a cupola, domed this time and closer to the front of the building. Larger than the previous courthouse, this structure had a pedimented portico at its main entrance as well as having at least one side entrance.

The current courthouse was completed in 1976 at a cost of approximately $1,100,000. It was designed by Hart, Freeland, and Roberts, Architects.

Left: Unicoi County's first courthouse. Center: The cupola of the 1915 courthouse now resides in a field, in use as a shed. Right: The second courthouse, completed in 1915.

UNION COUNTY

Formed: January 3, 1850
Formed from: Anderson, Campbell, Claiborne, Grainger, and Knox Counties
County seat: Maynardville
Area: 224 sq.mi.

Union County was named in response to the strong sentiment of the people of the region for the preservation of the Federal Union. However, there is another philosophy regarding the county name, stemming from the "strong sentiment of the people to unite portions of the counties."[1] The county seat, Maynardville (formerly Liberty), was named after Horace Maynard, a member of Congress who defended a suit against Union County by Knox County which delayed the organization of the county.[2]

The first court was held at the Liberty Meeting House in February 1854 until a brick courthouse was completed in 1858. This structure was torn down and rebuilt in 1900 as a two story brick structure with a corner stair tower and projecting entry porch. This courthouse burned in 1969.[3]

The current courthouse, the county's third, was finished in 1974 and occupies the original site. Until this courthouse was completed, the county used several locations for records and offices.

An early view of the 1900 courthouse.

VAN BUREN COUNTY

Formed: January 3, 1840
Formed from: Bledsoe, Warren, and White Counties
County seat: Spencer
Area: 274 sq.mi.

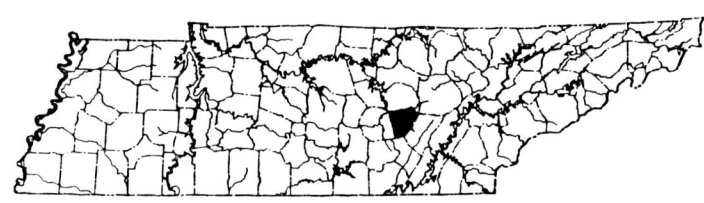

Van Buren County was named in honor of Martin Van Buren, governor of New York, Secretary of State to President Jackson, Vice President and later eighth President of the United States. Spencer, the county seat, was named for Thomas Sharp Spencer, who was killed by indians in this county.

In 1840 $100 was allocated for building a courthouse. It was apparently constructed of logs, with the contract being awarded to Andrew Parker.[1] Parker also donated 50 acres of land for the county seat.

The second courthouse, completed in 1855 was a two story brick structure, square in plan, which was used until 1906. The building had a low hip roof with a square cupola in the center. During that year the county decided to construct a new courthouse.

The current courthouse, again a nearly square, two story brick structure that has a hipped roof with a square cupola at the top was nearing completion when it was struck by a tornado in 1903. While destroying part of the courthouse, the damage was repaired and the courthouse was completed in 1904.[2]

A view of the third, current Van Buren County courthouse.

WARREN COUNTY

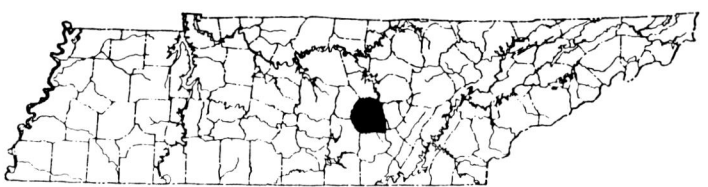

Formed: November 22, 1807
Formed from: White County
County seat: McMinnville
Area: 433 sq.mi.

Warren County was named for General Joseph Warren, a Revolutionary War veteran killed at the Battle of Bunker Hill. The first court met at the home of Joseph Westmoreland near Barren Fork (Tanyard Springs), where a 20 by 40 foot log courthouse was erected. This structure was in use for a little over two years, until the county seat moved to McMinnville in 1811.[1]

A permanent two story brick courthouse was constructed in the center of the public square in McMinnville sometime in 1811 by Capt. William White. This structure was very simple in design and had a hip roof with a center octagonal cupola.

The county later decided the public square was too small and purchased a new lot (no. 23) to the northeast of and fronting on the square. Plans for a new building were drawn by John E. Goodney. A two story brick Greek Revival design, it was completed in 1858 at a cost of $12,000. It was rectangular in plan with a gable roof. The design also included a center two story portico (later given a pediment). Once completed, it was found to have more space than the county needed and part of the second floor was leased out.[2]

The current courthouse, Warren County's fourth, was completed in 1897 at a cost of $18,000. This structure was located in the center of College Street. Designed by R.H. Hunt, this was a handsome two story brick structure that featured a four story tall corner clock tower, pyramid roofed corner pavilions and an arched central doorway.

The clock tower was lowered to three stories in 1954 (after being found to be in an unsafe condition). It now has a matching pyramid roof.

As originally constructed, the building did not have a basement. This area was excavated in the 1950s to accommodate a furnace and public restrooms. A two-story vault was added to the west side in 1959 and further additions were made in 1978, under H.T. Pelham.[3]

Left: Warren County's second courthouse (1811). Center: The third courthouse, completed in 1858. Right: The current courthouse with its original clock tower.

WASHINGTON COUNTY

Formed: November 1777
Formed from: The Washington District
County seat: Jonesborough
Area: 326 sq.mi.

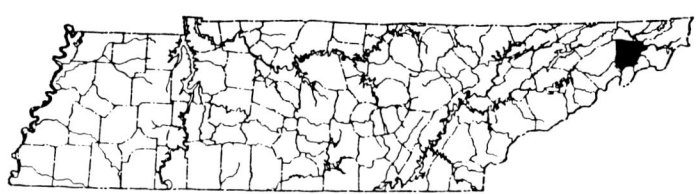

Washington County was named in honor of President George Washington and was the first political division in the United States to be named in his honor. Created by the North Carolina legislature, all other counties in Tennessee have been formed from this district. Jonesborough, the county seat, was named for Willie Jones, a North Carolina politician responsible for the planned community, which is the oldest town in the state. It was here that the State of Franklin was formed, with John Sevier as its first and only governor.

The initial three courthouses in the county were constructed of logs. The first was built in 1778 by Charles Robertson[1] of round logs covered with clapboards. A second was completed in 1784, with the following instructions: *...twenty-four feet square, diamond corner, and hewn down after it is built up; nine feet high between the floors, body of the upper floor, floors neatly laid with plank....* This was followed by a third in 1794, which was a two story log structure with the courtroom on the second floor. This was reached by a double flight of exterior stairs.[2] The jail was located on the first floor of this structure.

The fourth courthouse was a permanent brick structure completed in 1820. It burned in 1839, and a frame building on Main Street was used from 1839 until 1847, when a new courthouse was completed. This next structure cost $8,000 and was closely modeled on the Knox County courthouse. Typical of Jonesborough, it had stepped brick gable ends and a central cupola with clocks facing four directions. Taken over by the Confederate Army and used as a hospital,[3] it was badly deteriorated and was condemned after the War. However, it was renovated and continued in use until 1910.

The current courthouse, the county's seventh, was completed in 1912 and was modeled after the Blount County courthouse. Bauman and Bauman were the architects. The building was renovated and rededicated in 1988.

Left: The 1847 with a two story addition at one end.
Right: The 1847 courthouse being demolished.

WAYNE COUNTY

Formed: October 8, 1819
Formed from: Hickman and Humphreys Counties
County seat: Waynesboro
Area: 734 sq.mi.

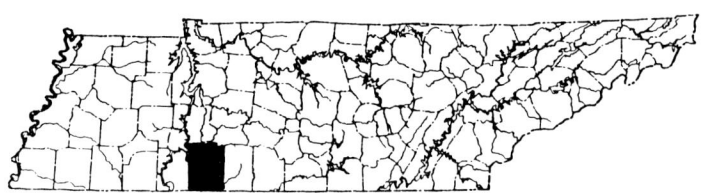

Wayne County was named for Major General Anthony Wayne, a Revolutionary War veteran. Initially created in 1817, the act creating the county was repassed in 1819. (An earlier Wayne County was established in 1785 and included the present Carter County and part of Johnson County. It was abolished in 1788.)

The first court met at Factor Fork, and later at William Barnett's home at Old Town on the Tom Branch, where a log courthouse was built. Waynesboro became the county seat in 1822. There, $800 was spent to erect a log courthouse with a dirt floor, board roof and large openings in the sides for windows. It was used until 1827. This was followed by a third courthouse which was 24 by 30 foot frame structure. It had offices on the first floor, a courtroom on the second, and had two entrances.[1]

The next courthouse was completed in 1844 to a design by architect Nathaniel Thomas, with D.G. Grimes and John Talley as builders. This was a two story brick structure, 35 by 40 feet and cost approximately $4,000. It was, in turn, replaced in 1905 by a two story concrete block courthouse designed by W.Chamberlin and Company. A Classical Revival style structure, it featured a pedimented central section with lower wings to either side. The design also incorporated a large domed clock tower in the center of its gable roof. Built at a cost of $25,000, it was destroyed by fire in 1973.[2]

The current courthouse, Wayne County's sixth, was completed in 1975. Of fireproof reinforced concrete construction, it was designed by Yearwood and Johnson architects of Nashville and was built by W.C. Moore Construction Company of Waynesboro at a cost $1,000,000.

Left: Wayne County's 1905 courthouse. Right: The fifth courthouse following the 1973 fire.

WEAKLEY COUNTY

Formed: October 21, 1823
Formed from: The Western District
County seat: Dresden
Area: 580 sq.mi.

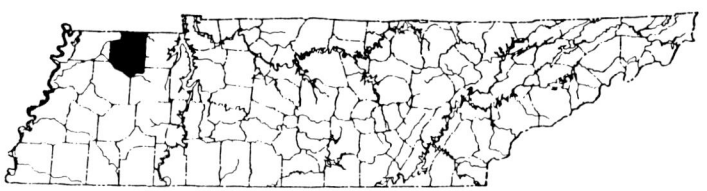

Weakley County was named for Colonel Robert Weakley, who represented Davidson County at the Constitutional Convention while it was still part of North Carolina, and was later a member of the Tennessee House of Representatives and member of the U.S. House of Representatives. The first courts were held in a small cabin, with no door, where sheep took over at night.[1]

John Terrell gave 39 acre of land for the county seat and the first permanent courthouse was completed in 1827. It was a brick structure, 40 feet square, built in the center of the court square by John Scarborough. It was demolished in 1852 when it became both too small and unsafe.

The next courthouse, completed in 1854, was a two story brick Greek Revival style structure with pilasters dividing each facade into three bays. It had a pyramid roofed tower located off-center on its low hip roof and contained two offices and a court room on each floor. Built at a cost of $20,000, two wings were later added during a 1911 renovation. It was destroyed by fire in 1948.

The current courthouse, the county's third, is a three story limestone structure costing $720,000. It was designed by Marr and Holman of Nashville in 1950, with Seth E. Giem and Associates of Memphis, the contractor. This three story stone clad structure is another example of Marr and Holman's severe Classical style [2]

Left: Weakley County's second (1854) courthouse. Right: Weakley County's current courthouse on completion in 1950.

WHITE COUNTY

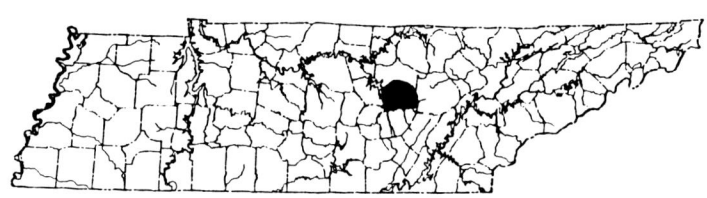

Formed: September 11, 1806
Formed from: Jackson, Overton and Smith Counties
County seat: Sparta
Area: 377 sq.mi.

White County was named for John White, veteran of the Revolutionary War and first settler in what later became White County. The first courts met at the home of Joseph Terry at Rock Island. A temporary log courthouse was erected and used for three years before Sparta was selected as the county seat in 1809.

A log courthouse erected at Sparta in 1810 was used until 1815, when a small square two story brick structure was erected[1]. This courthouse, costing $5,000, was used until 1894. It was a simple structure with a low hip roof, in the center of which was a square cupola with a steep pyramidal roof.

A third courthouse was completed in 1894. It was a large two story brick structure designed by Reuben H. Hunt. William E. Doolittle the contractor. This courthouse was an impressive structure which featured a tall square clock tower at one end. Typical of the late Victorian period, the exterior had projecting polygonal bays and elaborately detailed brickwork. The roof was a complicated mix of gables and polygonal turrets. It cost $13,000 and was used until 1974, when it was demolished.[2]

The current courthouse is White County's fourth. It was designed by Morton J. Lide of Birmingham, and Hardaway Construction Company was the contractor. This structure, a classically-inspired design faced in limestone, was completed at a cost of $1,000,000.

Left: White County's second courthouse, completed in 1815. Right: The third, 1894 courthouse.

WILLIAMSON COUNTY

Formed: October 26, 1799
Formed from: Davidson County
County seat: Franklin
Area: 582 sq.mi.

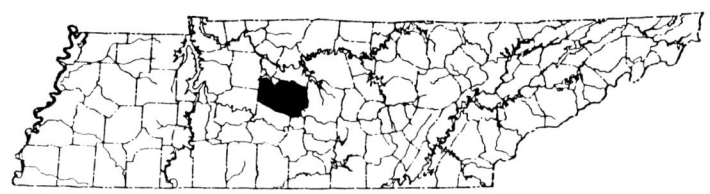

Williamson County was named for Dr. Hugh Williamson, colonel and surgeon general of the North Carolina Militia, and member of the Continental Congress. The county seat, Franklin, is named for his friend, Benjamin Franklin.

The first court met in McKay's log tavern. Within a year a log courthouse was built in the center of the public square. This was used until a more substantial structure was completed around 1809. Also located in the center of the public square, this second courthouse was a two story brick building with a small cupola on its roof. It was torn down in 1858 when the work on the new courthouse was well underway.[1]

The present courthouse, completed in 1859 at a cost of approximately $20,000, was built on the southeast corner of the public square. The building was completed under the supervision of John W. Miller of Franklin. It is a Greek Revival design featuring a center portico with four cast iron columns that were smelted in Fernvale and cast in a Franklin foundry. The design of this courthouse was apparently based on a similar structure in Lebanon.[2]

The courthouse was used as Federal headquarters during the Civil War and as a hospital after the Battle of Franklin. Interior renovations were undertaken in 1937, 1964 and 1976. Also in 1976, an annex was added to the rear of the structure.[3] The annex and the exterior restoration of the courthouse were designed by the Architectural office of Williams, Inc., of Franklin.

A view of the Williamson County courthouse c1950 when it was still painted white and had modern windows.

WILSON COUNTY

Formed: October 26, 1799
Formed from: Sumner County
County seat: Lebanon
Area: 571 sq.mi.

Wilson County was named for David Wilson, Revolutionary War veteran, member of the Territorial Assembly and speaker in its House of Representatives. Lebanon was selected as the county seat in 1802, the name coming from the biblical Lebanon because of the cedars growing around the area.

The first courthouse was a simple cedar log structure clad with riven oak clapboards. It had two jury rooms and a courtroom, but no offices. This was used until 1811, when it was replaced by a two story brick courthouse erected in the center of the public square. This building had a hipped roof with an square cupola. William Seawell built this structure for $500.[1]

The county's third courthouse was designed by William Strickland and was located on the south side of the square. Completed in 1848, it was a three story brick structure that featured full height corner pilasters, a low hip roof and a tall Corinthian order columned cupola. The circuit courtroom was located on the second floor, while county offices and the county courtroom were on the first floor. This building burned in 1881.

Courts were then held in the Odd Fellows Hall until the completion of the fourth courthouse in 1884. It was a large two story brick structure designed in the Second Empire style and was built by J.F. Bowers & Brothers Contractors of Nashville for $17,000. This design featured a brick portico and mansard roofs. It had tall first floor ceilings and two large courtrooms on the second floor. Enlarged in 1937, it was later remodelled in 1948 by architects Smith and Rome. By 1965 it was considered dilapidated and obsolete and was demolished.[2]

The current courthouse, Wilson County's fifth, is the first constructed off the public square. Designed by Morton-Carter Architects, it was completed for $1,200,000. The building is constructed of brick, concrete, glass block and steel.

Left: William Strickland's design for the third courthouse. Right: Wilson County's fourth, Second Empire style courthouse.

JAMES COUNTY

Formed: January 27, 1871 (dissolved 1919)
Formed from: Bradley and Hamilton Counties
County seat: Ooltewah
Area: ? sq.mi.

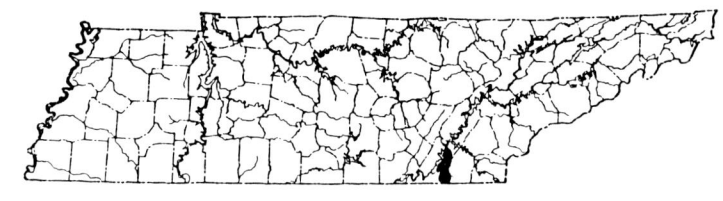

James County was organized during the troubled Reconstruction period, largely from the rural section of Hamilton County, where a rivalry between Harrison and Chattanooga eventually led to Chattanooga being selected as county seat in 1870. Legislation for the new county was introduced by Representative Elbert A. James of Hamilton County and it was named in honor of his father, Rev. Jesse J. James.[1]

Initially the new county used the old Hamilton County courthouse at Harrison, its first county seat. However, a permanent county seat was soon established at Ooltewah and this building was torn down. By 1893 Harrison had transferred back to Hamilton County after losing several bids to be the county seat.

The new courthouse completed in 1874 at Ooltewah was a three story brick structure designed by Hunt and Lamb, Architects, of Chattanooga.[2] It contained offices on the first floor, courtrooms on the second, and the W.A. Nelson Masonic Lodge No. 391 on the third. This courthouse burned in 1890.

Its replacement in 1892 was Romanesque style, two story brick structure trimmed with stone. It had a tall hipped roof and prominent, but squat roof tower. In 1913 it also burned.[3]

The third courthouse, erected in 1913 at a cost of $11,000, continued to be used until the county was dissolved in 1919. This building is a two story Neo-classical style brick structure with a wide pedimented portico. Listed on the National Register of Historic Places, this structure had been in use as a community center.[4]

Bottom: The second James County Courthouse at Ooltewah. Top: The third courthouse, still in use today, although no longer as a courthouse.

TENNESSEE COUNTY

Formed:	1788
Formed from:	Davidson County
County seat:	Clarksville
Area:	? sq.mi.

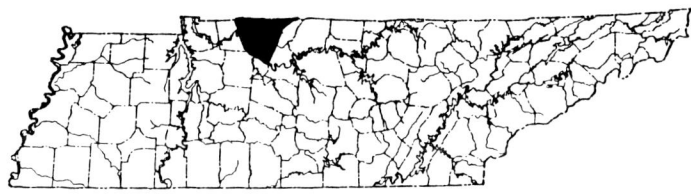

Tennessee County was formed in 1788 and apparently built a courthouse in Clarksville around 1790. However, this county was dissolved in 1796, when Robertson and Montgomery Counties were created at the time of Tennessee's statehood. The map from Joseph Scott's *The New and Universal Gazetteer* (Philadelphia, 1798-1800) shows the Mero District of Middle Tennessee (the "V" shape) and the approximate locations of the three counties formed there - Tennessee, Davidson and Sumner. Tennessee is the western-most of the three counties shown.

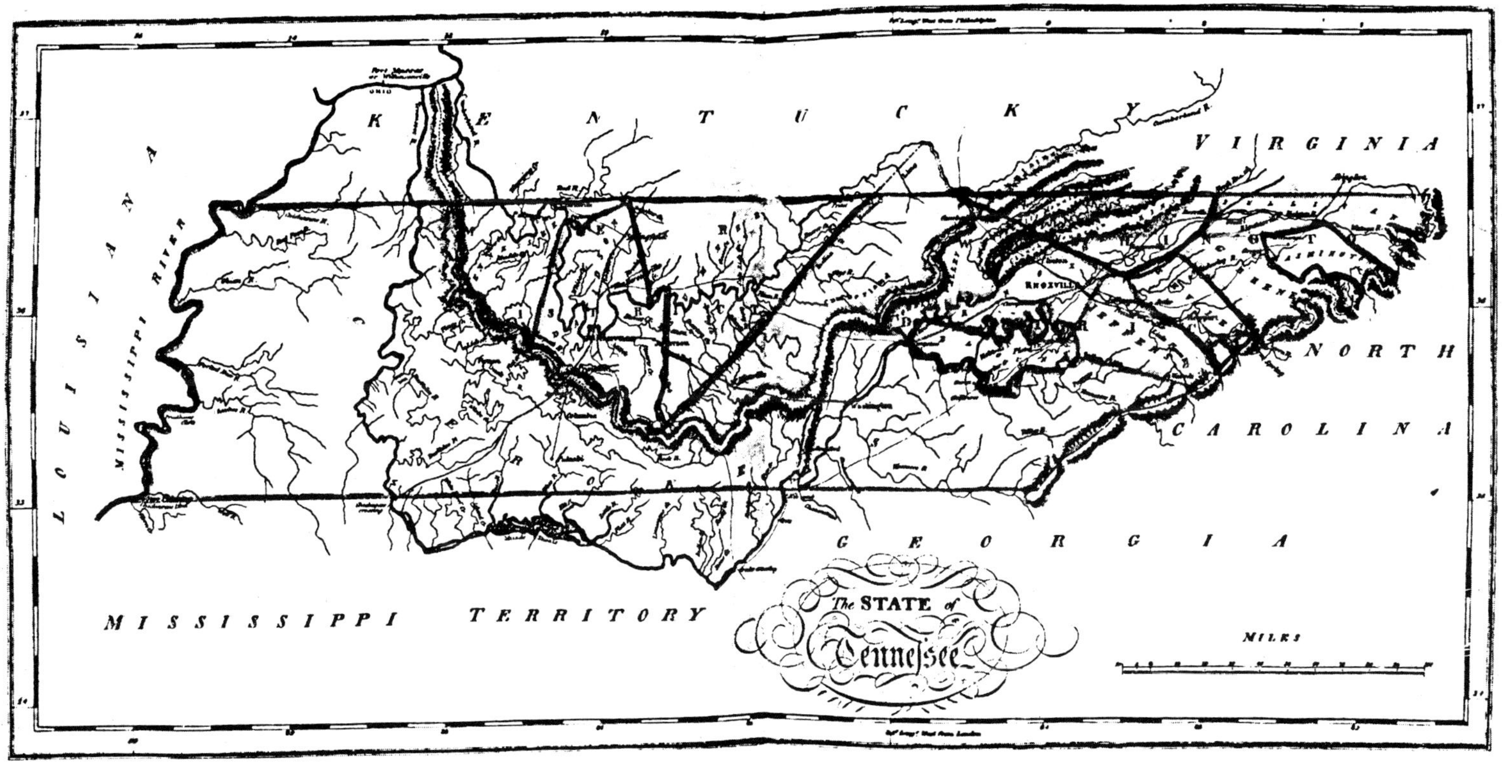

Dates of County Formation

By the State of North Carolina:

Year	Date	County
1777	November	Washington
1779		Sullivan
1783		Greene
1783	October 6	Davidson
1785		*Wayne - Abolished 1788*
1786		Hawkins
1786	November 17	Sumner
1788		*Tennessee - Dissolved April 9, 1796*
1792	June 11	Jefferson
1792	June 11	Knox
1794	September 27	Sevier
1795	July 11	Blount

By the State of Tennessee:

Year	Date	County
1796	April 9	Montgomery
1796	April 9	Robertson
1796	April	Carter
1796	July	Grainger
1797	October 9	Cocke
1799	October 26	Smith
1799	October 26	Williamson
1799	October 26	Wilson
1801	October 29	Claiborne
1801	November 6	Jackson
1801	December 3	Anderson
1801	December 13	Roane
1803	October 3	Dickson
1803	October 25	Rutherford
1803	November 1	Stewart
1806	September 11	Overton
1806	September 11	Campbell
1806	September 11	White
1807	November 22	Warren
1807	November 24	Maury
1807	November 30	Bledsoe
1807	November 30	Rhea
1807	December 3	Bedford
1807	December 3	Franklin
1807	December 3	Hickman
1809	October 19	Humphreys
1809	November 14	Giles
1809	November 14	Lincoln
1817	October 15	Morgan
1817	October 21	Lawrence
1817	November 20	Marion
1819	November 18	Monroe
1819	November 18	Perry
1819	October 8	Wayne
1819	October 25	Hamilton
1819	November 13	Hardin
1819	November 18	McMinn
1819	November 24	Shelby
1821	March 11	Carroll
1821	November 7	Henderson
1821	November 11	Henry
1821	November 11	Madison
1823	October 8	McNairy
1823	October 16	Dyer
1823	October 16	Hardeman
1823	October 21	Gibson
1823	October 21	Weakley
1823	October 24	Obion
1823	October 29	Tipton
1823	November 3	Haywood
1823	November 28	Fentress
1824	September 29	Fayette
1835	November 24	Benton
1835	November 24	Lauderdale
1836	January 2	Johnson
1836	January 8	Coffee
1836	January 20	Meigs
1836	January 21	Cannon
1836	February 10	Bradley
1836	February 26	Marshall
1837	December 11	Dekalb
1839	November 28	Polk
1840	January 3	Van Buren
1842	January 18	Macon
1843	December 23	Lewis
1844	January 7	Hancock
1844	January 29	Grundy
1845	November	Decatur
1849	December 17	Scott
1850	January 3	Union
1854	February 11	Putnam
1855	November 16	Cumberland
1856	February 28	Cheatham
1857	December 9	Sequatchie
1870	May 27	Loudon
1870	May 31	Hamblen
1870	June 9	Lake
1870	June 21	Trousdale
1870	December 7	Clay
1871	January 21	Houston
1871	*January 27*	*James - Disolved 1919*
1871	March 1	Chester
1871	November 23	Crockett
1871	December 14	Moore
1875	March 19	Unicoi
1879	February 25	Pickett

NOTES

Anderson County
1. GOOD87, p. 839.
2. GOOD87, p. 838.
3. HOSK79.
4. CRAN76, p. 1.

Bedford County
1. FOST23, p. 46.
2. GOOD87, p. 865.
3. GOOD87, p. 865.

Benton County
1. SMIT79, p. 33.
2. SMIT75, p. 72.

Bledsoe County
1. ROBN93, p. 191.
2. ROBN93, p. 191.

Blount County
1. GOOD80, p. 829-30.
2. GOOD80, p. 830.
3. GOOD80, p. 830.

Bradley County
1. LILL80, p. 67.
2. LILL80, p. 68.

Campbell County
1. FOST23, p. 9-10.
2. RIDE41, p. 24.
3. MCDO93, p. 27-29.
4. MCDO93, p. 31.
5. MCDO93, p. 34.
6. RIDE41, p. 86, 91.
7. MCDO93, p. 45.

Cannon County
1. FOST23, p. 47.
2. MASO92, p. 30.

Carroll County
1. FOST23, p. 102-103.
2. GOOD79, p. 800-801.
3. GOOD79, p. 801.

Carter County
1. GOOD80, p. 908.
2. GOOD80, p. 908.
3. CRAN76, p. 12.

Cheatham County
1. GOOD79, p. 953.
2. BINK80, p. 32-34.

Chester County
1. FOST23, p. 103.
2. GOOD87, p. 809.

Claiborne County
1. GOOD80, p. 847-48.
2. FOST23, p. 11.

Clay County
1. CCHH86, p. 13.
2. CCHH86, p. 32.

Cocke County
1. WALK76, p. 4.
2. personal communication, E.L. Walker III.
3. ODEL51.

Coffee County
1. FOST23, p. 51.
2. GOOD79, p. 831-832.
3. MCMA87, p. 73-80.

Crockett County
1. GOOD87, p. 833.
2. CCHS74, p. 10.

Cumberland County
1. KIWA82, p. 34.
2. FOST23, p. 12-13.

Davidson County
1. FOST23.

Decatur County
1. YOUNG78, p. 7.
2. YOUNG78, p. 18.
3. YOUN78, p. 18-19.
4. GOOD87, p. 815.
5. YOUN79, p. 92.

Dekalb County
1. WEBB95, p. 6.
2. WEBB86, p. 16-18.

Dickson County
1. GOOD87, p. 927.
2. CORL56, p. 32, 64.
3. HERN75, p. 138.

Dyer County
1. ALEX74, p.2.
2. FOST23, p. 105-106.
3. DCSE73, p. 3.
4. GOOD87, p. 845.

Fayette County
1. HERN75, p. 104.
2. MORT92, p. 21.
3. FAYE86, p. 246-47.
4. MORT89, p. 22.
5. FAYE86, p. 246-47.

Fentress County
1. FOST23, p. 57.
2. HOGU16, p. 2, 12.
3. HOGU16, p. 13.
4. FENT87, p. 53-55.

Franklin County
1. FCHR87, Vol. XVIII, No. 2, p. 59-65.
2. FCHR87, Vol. XVIII, No. 2, p. 65-89.

Gibson County
1. GREE01, p. 17-18.
2. GOOD87.
3. CULP61, p. 12-16.
4. HERN75, p. 162.
5. HERN75, p. 41.
6. CULP61, p. 12-16.
7. GREE01, p. 23.

Giles County
1. GREE01, p. 17-18.
2. GOOD87, p. ?.
3. CULP61, p. 12-16.
4. HERN75, p. 162.

Grainger County
1. GOOD80, p. 854-855.
2. FOST23, p. 13-14.
3. ROAC83, from "Grainger County in Days Gone By," 1962.
4. HOLT76, p. 6.
5. HOLT76, p. 6.

Greene County
1. GOOD80, p. 883-85.
2. CRAN76, p. 37.

Grundy County
1. FOST23, p. 61-62.

Hamblen County
1. HCCC70, p. 26-28.

Hamilton County
1. ARMS31, p. 96, 111, 116.
2. LIVI81, p. 236.
3. LIVI81, p. 314.

Hancock County
1. FOST23, p. 20-21.
2. HCHG89, p. 8.

Hardeman County
1. GOOD87, p. 821.
2. HCHC79, p. 8.
3. APTA88, "Historic Sites in Bolivar" brochure.
4. HERN75, p. Addendum.

Hardin County
1. GOOD87, p. 837.
2. BRAZ85, p. 7.
3. HCHQ72, p. 6
4. CRAN76, p. 44.

Hawkins County
1. FOST23, p. 21-22.
2. ROGA89, p. 23.

Haywood County
1. FOST23, p. 111-112.
2. WPAS39, p. 5.
3. GOOD87, p. 821.

Henderson County
1. GOOD87, p. 799.
2. POWE30, p. 30.
3. POWE30, p. 31.
4. BOLE22, p. ?.

Henry County
1. FOST23, p. 112-113.
2. BEDW87, p. 26-27.
3. INMA76, p. 5, 78-80.
4. JOHN58, p. 13.
5. HERN75, p. 99.

Hickman County
1. GOOD79, p. 792-793.

Houston County
1. MCCL66, p. 4-5.
2. GOOD87, p. 985.

Humphreys County
1. GARR63, p. 17.
2. WHIT79, p. 44.
3. WHIT79, p. 46-47.
4. GOOD87, p. 875.

Jackson County
1. TAYS89, p. 25.
2. TAYS89, p. 31-32.
3. TAYS89, p. 40.
4. Gainesboro Historic District National Register Nomination, 1990.

James County
1. DONN83, p. 3, 5-7.
2. HERN75, p. 99.
3. DONN83, p. 17-18.
4. DONN83, p. 22.

Jefferson County
1. GOOD80, p. 857-60.
2. HERN75, p. 94.

Johnson County
1. JCHS86, p. 12-13.

Knox County
1. GOOD87, p. 809.
2. GOOD87, p. 809-810.
3. HERN75, p. 52.
4. GOOD87, p. 812-813.

Lake County
1. LCHS93, p. 12.
2. LCHS93, p. 42.
3. LCHS93, p. 43.

Lauderdale County
1. PETE57, p. 72.
2. PETE57, p. 72.
3. CRAN76, p. 59.

Lawrence County
1. GOOD79, p. 752-753.
2. CARP86, p. 33-39, 85.

Lewis County
1. GOOD79, p. 803.

Lincoln County
1. MARS89, p. 54.
2. MARS89, p. 96.
3. MARS89, p. 64.
4. DICK77, p. 125-126.
5. DICK77, p. 71-72.

Loudon County
1. GOOD80, p. 827.

Macon County
1. FOST23, p. 68--69.
2. GOOD87, p. 835-838.
3. BLAN86, p. 27-31.
4. BLAN86, p. 27-31.

Madison County
1. GOOD80, p. 803-04.
2. WILL46, p. 38.
3. GOOD80, p. 803-04.
4. CRAN76, p. 67.
5. SCHW86, p. 115.

Marion County
1. MCHS90, p. 24-25.

Marshall County
1. MCHS86, p. 6-7.

Maury County
1. GARR86, p. 251-254.
2. GARR73, newspaper account, The Daily Herald, Feb. 15, 1973.
3. HERN75, p. 39.

McMinn County
1. GOOD80, p. 811.
2. FOST23, p. 27-28.
3. GOOD80, p. 811.
4. CRAN76, p. 64.

McNairy County
1. ADAMS52, p. 7.
2. ADAMS52, p. 9.
3. FOST23, p. 117-118.

Meigs County
1. GOOD80, p. 816.
2. FOST23, p. 29-30.
3. LILL75, p. 55.
4. LILL75, p. 55.
5. CRAN76, p. 72.

Monroe County
1. GOOD80, p. 807-08.
2. FOST23, p. 30-32.
3. SAND82, p. 535.
4. SAND82, p. 541
5. SAND82, p. 545.
6. SAND82, p. 547.
7. CRAN76, p. 73.

Montgomery County
1. BEAC64, p. 81.
2. BEAC64, p. 90.

Moore County
1. GOOD87, p. 807-809.

Morgan County
1. HERN75, p. 84.
2. FOST23, p. 32-33.

Obion County
1. MARS41, p. 28.
2. MARS41, p. 28.
3. MARS41, p. 29.
4. CRAN76, p. 79.

Overton County
1. ELDR76, p. 42.
2. CRAN76, p. 80.
3. OCHB92, p. 74-76.
4. ELDR76, p. 42.

Perry County
1. FOST23, p. 77-78.
2. GOOD87, p. 781-782.

Pickett County
1. HUDD73, p. 37.
2. PCBC91, p. 3.
3. Pickett County Press, 27 Feb 92.
4. Pickett County Press, 27 Feb 92.
5. CRAN76, p. 82.

Polk County
1. GOOD80, p. 805-06; Court term records, p. 12.
2. Court Term Records, p. 84.
3. CRAN76, p. 83.
4. BARC75, p. 105.

Putnam County
1. CRAN76, p. 84.

Rhea County
1. FOST23, p. 34-35.
2. GOOD80, p. 818.
3. CRAN76, p. 85.

Roane County
1. FOST23, p. 35-36.
2. GOOD80, p. 823-24.
3. CRAN76, p. 86-87.
4. HERN75, p. 84.
5. WILL82, p. 8.

Robertson County
1. AHM00, p. 313-25.
2. National Register Nomination for the Robertson County Courthouse.
3. CRAN76, p. 88-89.

Rutherford County
1. FOST23, p. 81-83.
2. RCBC76, p.?
3. CRAN76, p. 90-91.
4. TUCK78, p. 3.
5. TUCK78, p. 3-31.

Scott County
1. SMIT85, p. 417-420.
2. SAND74, p. 88.

Sequatchie County
1. FOST23, p. 38-39.

Sevier County
1. RAMS26, p. 295.
2. GOOD80, p. 834-35.
3. Knoxville Gazette, 23 Oct 1795.
4. GOOD80, p. 834-35.
5. CRAN76, p. 94-95.
6. Sevier County News-Record, 6 Nov 1969.
7. Knoxville News-Sentinel, 20, Sept 1970.

Shelby County
1. FOST23, p. 119-122.
2. GOOD87, p. 808-809.
3. HERN75, p. ?.
4. COPP76, p. 39-41.
5. HERN75, p. 45.
6. GOOD87, p.808-809.
7. HERN75, p. 76.

Smith County
1. SCHH86, p. 11.
2. MAGG86, p. 12.
3. FOST23, p. 83-84.
4. GOOD87, p. 824-827.
5. HERN75, p. 187.
6. HERN75, p. 163.
7. MAGG86, p. 13.

8. SCHH86, p. 13.

Stewart County
1. SCHS80, p. 8.
2. SCHS80, p. 16.
3. BRAN44, p. 16.

Sullivan County
1. GOOD80, p. 915.
2. HTCS93, p. 168.
3. HERN75, p. 55.
4. TAYL09, p. 92.
5. SPOD76, p. 122.

Sumner Couonty
1. GOOD87, p. 802-805.

Tipton County
1. BEAS81, p. 133-163.
2. BEAS81, p. 128.
3. BEAS81, p. 78.

Trousdale County
1. CRAN76, p. 104.
2. CRAN76, p. 104.

Unicoi County
1. CRAN76, p. 105.

Union County
1. Peters, correspondence with, 8/15/94.
2. FOST23, p. 43-44.
3. THAR85

Van Buren County
1. MEDL87, p. 105.
2. MEDL87, p. 287.

Warren County
1. GOOD87, p. 816-818; Dillon, Warren County News, 1981.
2. WOMA60, p. 34-35.
3. WOMA60, p. 36.

Washington County
1. FOST23, p. 44-45.
2. GOOD80, p. 895.
3. WATA88, p. 158-159.

Wayne County
1. WCHS, p. 77.
2. CRAN76, p. 112.

Weakley County
1. FOST23
2. VAUG83, p. 17-20.

White County
1. GOOD87, p. 801-802.
2. ROGE72, p. 3-5.

Williamson County
1. BOWM71, p. 130-131.
2. HERN75, p. 133.
3. Tennessee Historical Commission historical marker.

Wilson County
1. BURN83, p. 19-20.
2. MERR61, p. 44-45.

Other Notes
p. viii PARE78: Paul C. Reardon, "Origins and Impact of the County Court System,", p. 19-33.

PHOTO CREDITS

Major photographic sources & notes:
TSLA: Tennessee State Library & Archives
TSLA/LB: TSLA, "Looking Backward at Tennessee" photo collection
MC: McClung Collection, Knxoville, TN
ME: Author's collection/drawing
CD: Colonial Dames Courthouse Survey (see Bibliography)
JC: John Carpenter
nn: no number or related catalogue information
co: courtesy of/collection of

Tennessee's County Courthouses
vii   ME
viii ME
ix   TSLA/LB, SU190
x   tl: COLE94
      bl: BHCH89
      tr: DICK77
      br: MARI90
xi   l: TSLA, nn
      c: KREC56
      r: WHIT79, p.20
xii   l: ME
      c: TSLA, 5387
      r: PATR81, co: Harlan Klepper
xiii tl: CD
      bl: PATR81, Michael Tomlan photographc
      tr: TSLA/LB, HB080
      br: SCH87, p. 800, c1950s
xiv   l: CD
      c: HOSK79, p. 104
      tr: Daily Herald, 2/15/73, dedication ceremony 1906
      br: MC
xv   tl: ME
      bl: ME
      r: JC

Tennessee and Its State Capitols
xx   l: TSLA 408
      c: Rocky Mount Historical Association
      r: Blount Mansion Association
xxi   tl: ME
      bl: TSLA/THS III F4 Box 3 #8: photo by G.F. Steinwehr, Rockwood, 1889
      r: Illustration from Crew's *History of Nashville*, c1880.
xxii t: TSLA 2029
      b: TSLA 1257, c1860
xxiii tc: TSLA, wood engraving: H. Bosse *Nashville City and Business Directory for 1860-61*
      bc: ME
      bl: ME
xxiv *Tennessee Blue Book 1995-1996 Bicentennial Edition*

Anderson County
1. l: TSLA, nn
2. r: CD, newspaper photo

Bedford County
1. TSLA 6278a

Benton County
1. l: TSLA 5159
2. r: SMIT79, p. 34

Bledsoe County
1. l: TSLA/LB SQ141, 1909 fire
2. r: TSLA/LB SQ050

Blount County
1. l: TIND73, p. 16, 1839
2. c: TIND73, p. 17, 1882
3. r: MC: Knoxville, Box 3

Bradley County
1. l: LILL76, p. 151
2. r: TSLA/LB BR038, c1930

Campbell County
1. l: TSLA 5533
2. r: JC

Cannon County
1. l: TSLA/LB CA090, 1935, co: Violet Hite
2. c: MASO82, p. 32
3. r: TSLA/LB CA091, 1936

Carroll County
1. l: TSLA 5644
2. r: TSLA/LB, HF079

Carter County
1. l: TSLA/LB CR145, 1880
2. r: ME

Chester County
1. TSLA 5522

Claiborne County
1. Holt81, p. 61

Clay County
1. l: TSLA/LB, L050, 1923
2. r: ME

Cocke County
1. l: ODELL51
2. r: NCCM85, p. 119, co: Mary Louise Nodell

Coffee County
1. l: MART69, co: George Chumbley
2. r: TSLA/LB CF136, 1896

Crockett County
1. l: TSLA 5018
2. r: MC, Box 2

Cumberland County
1. l: TSLA 5316
2. r: ME

Davidson County
1. l: TSLA, THS (III F-4, Box 4 #9)
2. tc: TSLA 5893, 1894
3. bc: TSLA/LB WL216, 1924
4. r: ME

Decatur County
1. l: TSLA 5357a
2. r: YOUNG78, p. 28

Dekalb County
1. l: WEBB95, p. 8
2. c: CD
3. r: WEBB95, p. 371

Dickson County
1. TSLA nn

Dyer County
1. l: HULM82, p.4
2. c: CD
3. r: MC, Knoxville, Box 2

Fayette County
1. MORT89, p. 23

Fentress County
1. l: FENT87
2. c: FENT87
3. r: FENT87, p. 57

Franklin County
1. CD

Gibson County
1. l: GREE01, p. 18
2. r: GREE01, p. 23, 1901

Giles County
1. l: ME
2. r: TSLA/LB GI221

Grainger County
1. t: TSLA 6241
2. b: GCBC76, p.3

Greene County
1. l: TSLA, nn
2. r: TSLA/LB SU265, 1917

Grundy County
1. l: NICH82, p. 22
2. r: Nashville Banner, 5/5/92.

Hamblen County
1. l: MC, Box 3
2. r: HCCC70, p. 28

Hamilton County
1. l: ARMS31, between p. 98-99
2. r: TSLA, 5214

Hancock County
1. HCHG89, p. 69, 1910

Hardeman County
1. l: Don Shackelford
2. r: TSLA 1418

Hardin County
1. l: TSLA/LB HD128, 1870
2. r: TSLA/LB HD121, 1907

Hawkins County
1. PATC81, p.98

Haywood County
1. HACH89, p. 235, c1899

Henderson County
1. l: STEW79, p. 59
2. r: POWE30, frontispiece

Henry County
1. r: TSLA 6712
2. l: TSLA/LB HE152, 1896

Hickman County
1. TSLA 5180

Houston County
1. l: MCCL66
2. r: TSLA 5404

Humphreys County
1. l: WHIT79, p. 20
2. r: The Photo Shop,

Jackson County
1. l: TSLA 5480
2. r: TSLA/LB JK051, c1900

James County
1. b: DUNN83, p. 165, 1913
2. t: JC

Jefferson County
1. l: TSLA/LB JF054, c1900
2. c: BIBL91, p. 16
3. r: TSLA/LB JF053, c1900

Johnson County
1. JCHB89, p. 13, 1894

Knox County
1. l: PATC81, p130 #144
2. r: TSLA, nn

Lake County
1. LCHS93, p. 42 co: Maggie Campbell

Lauderdale County
1. l: TSLA/LB L170, ca1890
2. c: TSLA/LB L056, c1912
3. r: ME

Lawrence County
1. l: CARP86, p. 19
2. r: Postcard from courthouse Register of Deeds collection

Lewis County
1. TSLA 5618

Lincoln County
1. l: TSLA, nn, co: T.V. McCowan
2. r: DICK77, 1936

Loudon County
1. CD

Macon County
1. BLAN86, p.28

Madison County
1. l: WILL46, c1870
2. r: TSLA, 5529

Marion County
1. l: MARI90, p.3
2. c: ME
3. r: MARI90, p.3

Marshall County
1. l: MCHB86, p. 6
2. r: TSLA/LB MS158, 1931

Maury County
1. l: TSLA nn
2. r: TSLA, 353

McMinn County
1. r: BYRU84, p. 71
2. l: BYRU84

McNairy County
1. l: WHIT73, p. 65
2. r: WHIT73, p. 55

Meigs County
1. l: TSLA, nn
2. c: LILL75
3. r: LILL75

Monroe County
1. SAND82, p.564, sketch by C.F. Hunt, 1955
2. CD

Montgomery County
1. r: Clarksville/Montgomery County Museum collection
2. l: TSLA/LB MT081, 1900

Moore County
1. CD

Morgan County
1. l: DICK87, p. 43, 1870 (TSLA)
2. r: TSLA/LB MG023, 1970s

Obion County
1. l: MARS41, after p. 270
2. c: copy of architect's drawing co: R.C. Forrester
3. r: CD

Overton County
1. TSLA 5387

Perry County
1. TSLA 591

Pickett County
1. l: TSLA 5151
2. r: PCBH91, p. 9

Polk County
1. l: TSLA 5124
2. r: co: Marian Presswood

Putnam County
1. TSLA, nn

Rhea County
1. l: CD
2. r: TSLA/LB, RH070

Roane County
1. l: WILL82
2. r: MC, Box 3

Robertson County
1. l: postcard co: Yolanda Reid
2. r: ME

Rutherford County
1. l: RCBC76
2. r: RCBC76

Scott County
1. l: SAND74, p. 24, 1874
2. c: TSLA/LB SC130, c1909
3. tr: TSLA/LB SC127, c1917
4. br: SAND74, p. 24, 1948

Sequatchie County
1. l: TSLA, nn
2. r: TSLA/LB, SQ050

Sevier County
1. t: Sevier County history
2. b: photo by Edmon Patterson, c1894

Shelby County
1. l: CD
2. r: TSLA 5763

Smith County
1. l: ME
2. r: SCHH86, p. 12

Stewart County
1. TSLA, Garrett: VII-C-3,4,5/ac. no. 68-338

Sullivan County
1. l: HTGS93, p. 171
2. r: HTGS93, p. 171

Sumner County
1. l: TSLA/LB, SU166
2. c: DURH86, p. 104, #180
3. r: ME

Tipton County
1. l: BEAS81, p. 78
2. r: TSLA/LB, TP141

Trousdale County
1. l: MCMU70, p.102
2. r: TCHS85, p.78

Unicoi County
1. r: TSLA/LB CR329, c1900
2. c: JC
3. l: TSLA, nn

Union County
1. GRAV78, p. 129, c129

Van Buren County
1. MEDL87, p. 298, c1918 (TSLA)
2. MEDL87, p. 282

Warren County
1. l: co: Dillon, county historian
2. c: TSLA/LB WA082, c1880
3. r: TSLA/LB WA089, 1897

Washington County
1. l:
2. r: TSLA/LB CR062, 1911

Wayne County
1. l: TSLA nn, photo by Lovic Meredith
3. r: co: Richard Quinn, 1972

Weakley County
1. l: TSLA 5387
2. r: ME

White County
1. l: TSLA/LB WH041, c1880
2. r: TSLA/LB WH038, c1912

Williamson County
1. CD

Wilson County
1. Tennessee State Museum
2. CD

BIBLIOGRAPHY

GENERAL

CRAN76 Crane, Sophie and Paul. *Tennessee Taproots.* Old Hickory, TN: Earle-Shields Publishers, 1976.

DILT91 Dilts, Jon. *The Magnificent 92: Indiana Courthouses.* Bloomington, IN: Rose Bud Press, 1991.

FOST23 Foster, Austin P. *Counties of Tennessee.* Nashville: State of Tennessee, 1923

GOOD87 Goodspeed Publishing Co. *History of Tennessee, Illustrated.* Nashville: Goodspeed Publishing Co., 1887.
- Bedford, Marshall, Maury, Rutherford, Williamson, and Wilson Counties
- Benton, Carroll, and Henry Counties
- Dyer, Gibson, Lake, Obion, and Weakley Counties
- Henderson, Chester, McNairy, Decatur, and Hardin Counties
- Lauderdale, Tipton, Haywood, and Crockett Counties

GOOD79 Goodspeed Publishing Co. *History of Tennessee Illustrated.* Reprint, TN: Southern Historical Press, 1979.
- Cannon, Coffee, DeKalb, Warren, and White Counties
- Fayette and Hardeman Counties
- Giles, Lincoln, Franklin, and Moore Counties
- Hamilton, Knox, and Shelby Counties
- Lawrence, Wayne, Perry, Hickman, and Lewis Counties
- Montgomery, Robertson, Humphreys, Stewart, Dickson, Cheatham, and Houston Counties
- Sumner, Smith, Macon, and Trousdale Counties
- Madison

GOOD80 Goodspeed Publishing Co. *History of Tennessee Illustrated: Containing Historical and Biographical Sketches of Thirty East Tennessee Counties.* Reprint, TN: Southern Historical Press, 1979.
- Anderson, Bledsoe, Blount, Bradley, Campbell, Carter, Cocke, Claiborne, Grainger, Greene, Hamblen, Hancock, Hawkins, James, Jefferson, Johnson, Loudon, McMinn, Meigs, Monroe, Morgan, Polk, Rhea, Roane, Sevier, Sullivan, Union, Unicoi, Washington, Knox, Hamilton.

HERN75 Herndon, Joseph L. *Architects in Tennessee Until 1930: A Dictionary.* New York: Master's Thesis, Columbia University, 1975.

PAIN01 Paine, Thomas H. *Short Sketches of the Counties of Tennessee.* Nashville: Tennessee Dept. of Agriculture, 1901.

PARE78 Pare, Richard (editor). *Courthouse: A Photographic Document.* New York: Horizon Press, 1978.

PATR81 Patrick, James. *Architecture in Tennessee: 1768-1897.* Knoxville: University of Tennessee Press, 1981.

SCHW86 Schweitzer, George K. *Tennessee Geneaological Research.* Knoxville: Private Printing, 1986.

THS81 Tennessee Historical Commission. "Tennessee Capitol Cities and the Tennesse State Capitol." Nashville, State printing office, 1981.

ANDERSON COUNTY

GOOD87 "Anderson County." *History of Tennessee.* East Tennessee Edition, ed. Weston A. Goodspeed et al., pp. 837-40, 1104-23. Nashville: Goodspeed Publishing, 1887.

HOSK79 Hoskins, Katherine B. *Anderson County.* Tennessee County History Series, Memphis: Memphis State University Press, 1979.

SEEB28 Seeber, Raymond C. *A History of Anderson County, Tennessee.* Knoxville: Thesis, University of Tennessee, 1928.

WPAS41 Historical Records Survey, Tennessee. *Inventory of the County Archives of Tennessee: Anderson County.* Nashville: The Survey;, WPA, 1941.

BEDFORD COUNTY

GOOD86 "Bedford County." *History of Tennessee,* ed. Weston A. Goodspeed et al., pp. 861-84, 1126-89. Nashville: Goodspeed Publishing, 1886.

DAVI77 Davidson, H. Lewis. *History of Bedford County.* Chattanooga: W.I. Crandall, 1877.

WPAS40 Historical Records Survey, Tennessee. *Inventory of the County Archives of Tennessee: Bedford County.* Nashville: The Survey, WPA, 1940.

BENTON COUNTY

GOOD87 "Benton County." *History of Tennessee,* ed. Weston A. Goodspeed et al., pp;. 832-46, 935-54. Nashville: Goodspeed Publishing, 1887.

SMIT70 Smith, Johnathan K. *A History of Benton County, Tennessee to 1900.* Memphis: J. Edge Co., 1970.

SMIT75 Smith, Jonathan K.T. Esq. *Historic Benton: A People's History of Benton County, Tennessee.* Memphis: Richard A. Harris Printer, 1975.

SMIT79 Smith, Jonathan K.T. Esq. *Benton County.* Tennessee County History Series. Memphis: Memphis State University Press, 1979.

BLEDSOE COUNTY

GOOD87 "Bledsoe County." *History of Tennessee,* East Tennessee Edition, ed. Weston A. Goodspeed et al., pp. 1071

ROBN57 Robnett, Elizabeth P. "A History of Bledsoe County, Tennessee: 1807-1957." Nashville: Ed.S. Dissertation, George Peabody College, 1957.

ROBN93 Robnett, Elizabeth P. *Bledsoe County, Tennessee: A History.* Signal Mountain, TN: Mountain Press, 1993.

BLOUNT COUNTY

GOOD87 "Blount County." *History of Tennessee,* East TN Ed., ed. Weston A. Goodspeed et al., pp. 828-33, 1088-96. Nashville: Goodspeed Publishing, 1887.

BURN57 Burns, Inez, E. *History of Blount County, Tennessee.* Nashville: Benson Printing Co., 1957.

SMIT91 Smith, Lorene B. and Elgin P. Kinter. *Blount County Remembered: The Photography of W.O. Garner.* Maryville, TN: Blount County Genealogical and Historical, Society, 1991.

TIND73 Tindell, Ted. *Blount County, Communities We Live In.* Maryville, TN: Brazos Press, 1973.

WPAS73 Historical Records Survey, Tennessee. *Inventory of the County Archives of Tennessee: Blount County.* Nashville: The Survey, WPA, 1941.

BRADLEY COUNTY

CCOC29 Cleveland Chamber of Commerce. *Bradley County, Tennessee.* (2 vols.) Cleveland: Historical & Pictorial Advertising, 1929.

GOOD87 "Bradley County." *History of Tennessee,* East Tennessee Edition, ed. Weston A. Goodspeed et al., pp. 798-804, 962-87. Nashville: Goodspeed Publishing, 1887.

LILL76 Lillard, Roy G. (Editor). *The History of Bradley County.* Cleveland, TN: Bradley Co. Chapter, East Tennessee Historical Society, 1976.

LILL80 Lillard, Roy G. *Bradley County.* Tennessee County History Series, Memphis: Memphis State University Press, 1980.

SHEL86 Shell, William R. *Cleveland The Beautiful: A History of Cleveland, Tennessee, 1842-1931.* Nashville: Williams Printing Company, 1986.

SLAY67 Slay, James L. "A History of Bradley County, Tennessee to 1861." Knoxville: Master's Thesis, University of Tennessee, 1967.

WOOT49 Wooten, John Morgan. *A History of Bradley County.* Cleveland: Bradley Co. Post 81, American Legion, with the Tennessee Historical Commission, 1949.

WPAS41 Historical Records Survey, Tennessee. Inventory of the County Archives of Tennessee: Bradley County. Nashville: The Survey, WPA, 1941.

CAMPBELL COUNTY

GOOD87 "Campbell County." *History of Tennessee,* East Tennessee Edition, ed. Weston A. Goodspeed et al., pp. 844-46, 1125-35. Nashville: Goodspeed Publishing, 1887.

MCDO93 McDonald, Miller. *Campbell County, Tennessee, USA.* LaFollette, TN: County Services Syndicate, 1993.

RIDE41 Ridenour, George L. *The Land of the Lake: A History of Campbell County, Tennessee.* LaFollette, TN: LaFollette Publishers, 1941.

CANNON COUNTY

BROW36 Brown, Sterling Spurlock. *History of Woodbury and Cannon County, Tennessee.* Manchester, TN: Doak Printing Co., 1936.

GOOD87 "Cannon County." *History of Tennessee.* ed. Weston A. Goodspeed et al., pp. 854-60, 987-92. Nashville: Goodspeed Publishing, 1887.

MASO82 Mason, Robert L. *Cannon County.* Tennessee County History Series, Memphis: Memphis State University Press, 1982.

MASO84 Mason, Robert L. *History of Cannon County, Tennessee.* Murfreesboro, TN: Lancer Printing Co., 1984.

CARROLL COUNTY

CARR72 Carroll County Historical Society. *Carroll County.* TN: Private Printing, 1972.

GOOD87 Carroll County." *History of Tennessee.* ed. Weston A. Goodspeed et al., pp. 797-813, 847-88. Nashville: Goodspeed Publishing, 1887.

DEVA72 De Vault, Mary Ruth. *Carroll County Sesquicentennial Booklet.* McKenzie, TN: McKenzie Banner, 1972.

CARTER COUNTY

GOOD87 "Carter County." *History of Tennessee,* East Tennessee Edition, ed. Weston A. Goodspeed et al., pp. 906-12, 1289-99. Nashville: Goodspeed Publishing, 1887.

MERR50 Merritt, Frank. *Early History of Carter County, 1760-1861.* Knoxville: East Tennessee Historical Society, 1950.

CHEATHAM COUNTY

BINK80 Binkley, Lois Barnes. *The Deserted Sycamore Village of Cheatham County.* TN: Private Printing, 1980.

GOOD87 "Cheatham County." *History of Tennessee.* ed. Weston A. Goodspeed et al., pp. 947-74, 1358-88. Nashville: Goodspeed Publishing, 1887.

WPA41 Historical Records Survey, Tennessee. *Inventory of the County Archives of Tennessee: Cheatham County.* Nashville: The Survey, WPA, 1941.

CHESTER COUNTY

GOOD87 "Chester County." *History of Tennessee.* ed. Weston A. Goodspeed et al., pp. 806-13, 862-69. Nashville: Goodspeed Publishing, 1887.

HEND60 Henderson Area Centennial. *Henderson Centennial Celebration Commemorating 100 Years of Progress: From Indians to Industry.* Jackson, TN: Laycock, 1960.

REID67 Reid, Mrs. S. E. *A Brief History of Chester County, Tennessee, Then and Now. An Historical Comparison, Facts of the Past and Present Which the Future Will Want to Remember.* Jackson, TN: McCowat-Mercer Press, 1924, 1967.

CLAIBORNE COUNTY

GOOD87 "Claiborne County." *History of Tennessee,* East Tennessee Edition ed. Weston A. Goodspeed et al., pp. 847-50, 1136-45. Nashville: Goodspeed Publishing, 1887.

HOLT81 Holt, Edgar A. *Claiborne County.* Tennessee County History Series, Memphis: Memphis State University Press, 1981.

CLAY COUNTY

CCHH86 Clay County Homecoming '86 Historical Book Committee. *Clay County Tennessee, 1986.* Paducah, KY: Turner Publishing Co., 1986.

STON62 Stone, William Curtis. "Historical Sketches of Clay County, Tennessee." Unpublished typescript, 1962.

COCKE COUNTY

GOOD87 "Cocke County." *History of Tennessee*, East Tennessee Edition ed. Weston A. Goodspeed et al., pp. 864-67, 1194-99. Nashville: Goodspeed Publishing, 1887.

ODEL51 O'Dell, Ruth Webb. *Over the Misty Blue Hills: The Story of Cocke County, Tennessee*. Newport (?), 1951.

WALK76 Walker, E.R. III. *Cocke County: A Thumbnail Sketch*. TN: Private Printing, 1976.

COFFEE COUNTY

GOOD87 "Coffee County." *History of Tennessee*. ed. Weston A. Goodspeed et al., pp. 827-45, 921-51. Nashville: Goodspeed Publishing, 1887.

EWEL36 Ewell, Leighton. *A History of Coffee County, Tennessee*. Manchester, TN: Doak Printing Co., 1936.

MART69 Martinze, Corinne. *Coffee County from Arrowheads to Rockets*. Tullahoma, TN: Coffee County Conservation Board, 1969.

MCMA83 McMahan, Basil B. *Coffee County, Tennessee Then and Now*. Nashville: Williams Printing Co., 1983.

CROCKETT COUNTY

CCHS74 Crockett County Historical Society. *Crockett County Courthouse Centennial*. Jackson, TN: Tennessee Industrial Printing Services, Inc., 1974.

GOOD87 "Crockett County." *History of Tennessee*. ed. Weston A. Goodspeed et al., pp. 830-42, 947-71. Nashville: Goodspeed Publishing, 1887.

WPAS36 Historical Records Survey, Tennessee. *Inventory of the County Archives of Tennessee: Crockett County*. Nashville: The Survey, WPA, 1936.

CUMBERLAND COUNTY

KIWA82 Kiwanis Club of Crab Orchard. *A Short History of Cumberland County*. Private re-printing, 1982.

KREC56 Krechniak, Helen Bullard and Joseph M. *Cumberland County's First Hundred Years*. Nashville: Crossville Centennial Commission, 1956.

DAVIDSON COUNTY

CLAY71 Clayton, W. Woodford. *History of Davidson County, Tennessee, with Illustrations and Biographical Sketches of Its Prominent Men and Pioneers*. (Reprint of 1880 ed.) Nashville: Charles Elder, 1971.

CREI69 Creighton, Wilbur Foster. *Building of Nashville*. Nashville: Private Printing, 1969.

DEKL66 Dekle, Clayton B. "The Tennessee State Capitol." *Tennessee Historical Quarterly*, vol 25 (1966), pp. 213-38.

EGER79 Egerton, John. *Nashville: The Faces of Two Centuries*. Nashville: PlusMedia Inc., 1979.

DECATUR COUNTY

GOOD87 "Decatur County." *History of Tennessee*. ed. Weston A. Goodspeed et al., pp. 814-19, 880-94. Nashville: Goodspeed Publishing, 1887.

YOUN78 Younger, Lillye. *The History of Decatur County, Past and Present*. Southaven, MS: Carter Printing Co., 1978.

YOUN79 Younger, Lillye. *Decatur County*. Tennessee County History Series. Memphis: Memphis State University Press, 1979.

DEKALB COUNTY

GOOD87 "DeKalb County." *History of Tennessee*. ed. Weston A. Goodspeed et al., pp. 845-53, 951-87. Nashville: Goodspeed Publishing, 1887.

HALE15 Hale, Will T. *History of DeKalb County, Tennessee*. Nashville: Paul Hunter Publisher, 1915.

SDCC89 Smithville-Dekalb Co. Chamber of Commerce. *A Pictorial Sampling of Dekalb County, Tennessee*. Nashville: Taylor Publishing Co. 1989.

WEBB86 Webb, Thomas G. *DeKalb County*. Tennessee County History Series. Memphis: Memphis State University Press, 1986.

WEBB95 Webb, Thomas G. *A Bicentennial History of DeKalb County*. Smithville, TN: Bradley Printing Co., 1995.

DICKSON COUNTY

CORL56 Corlew, Robert Ewing. *A History of Dickson County, Tennessee*. Nashville: Tennessee Historical Commission and the Dickson County Historical Commission, 1956.

GOOD87 "Dickson County." *History of Tennessee*. ed. Weston A. Goodspeed et al., pp. 920-47, 1329-57. Nashville: Goodspeed Publishing, 1887.

DYER COUNTY

ALEX74 Alex , . *Dyer County: The Garden Spot of the World*. Dyersburg, TN: Wallace Printing Co., 1974.

GOOD87 "Dyer County." *History of Tennessee*. ed. Weston A. Goodspeed et al., pp. 842-52, 1024-73. Nashville: Goodspeed Publishing, 1887.

DCSE73 *Dyer County Sesquicentennial: 1823-1973*. Newbern, TN: Anderson Printing Co., 1973.

HULM82 Hulme, Albert L. and James A. (Editors). *A History of Dyer County*. TN: Private Printing.

HULM85 Hulme, Albert L. *Dyer County Vol. II. Past and Present: A Pictorial History of Dyer County*. Dyersburg, TN: Wallace Printing Co., 1985.

FAYETTE COUNTY

GOOD87 "Fayette County." *History of Tennessee*. ed. Weston A. Goodspeed et al., pp. 797-817, 840-87. Nashville: Goodspeed Publishing, 1887.

FAYE74 Fayette County Sesquicentennial, Inc. *150 Years in Fayette County, Tennessee; 1824-1874*. TN: Private Printing.

FAYE86 Fayette County Historical Society. *The History of Fayette County, Tennessee*. Salem, WV: Walsworth Press, 1986.

MORT89 Morton, Dorothy Rich. *Fayette County*. Tennessee County History Series, Memphis: Memphis State University Press, 1989.

FENTRESS COUNTY

FENT87 Fentress Co. Historical Society. *History of Fentress County, Tennessee*. Dallas: Curtis Media Corp., 1987.

HOGU16 Hogue, A.R. *History of Fentress County*. Nashville: Williams Printing Co., 1916.

FRANKLIN COUNTY

GOOD87 "Franklin County." *History of Tennessee*. ed. Weston A. Goodspeed et al., pp. 7785-804, 820-46. Nashville: Goodspeed Publishing, 1887.

RHOT41 Rhoton, Thomas Foster. "A Brief History of Franklin County, Tennessee." Knoxville: Master's Thesis, University of Tennessee, 1941.
ROGE86 Rogers, Evelyn. *Focus on Franklin County*. TN: Private Printing, 1986.
FCHR87 Sons, Charles. *"The Courthouses of Franklin County,"* Franklin County Historical Review, Vol. XVIII, No. 2, 1987, p. 59-70.

GIBSON COUNTY

CULP61 Culp, Frederick M. and Mrs. Robert E. Ross. *Gibson County: Past and Present.* Jackson, TN: Gibson County Historical Society, 1961.
GOOD87 "Gibson County." *History of Tennessee.* ed. Weston A. Goodspeed et al., pp. 797-816, 857-931. Nashville: Goodspeed Publishing, 1887.
GREE01 Greene, W.P. *Gibson County, Tennessee: A Series of Pen and Picture Sketches.* Nashville: Gospel Advocate Publishing Co., 1901.
SMIT60 Smith, Conrad F. *The Gibson County Story. A Historical Drama of Gibson County, Tennessee, from Indian Times through Eventful, Tragic and Romantic Years of War and Peace to the Present.* Trenton, TN: Herald-Register, 1960.

GILES COUNTY

COHE51 Cohen, Nelle Roller. *Pulaski History, 1809-1950: the Beginning, the Building, the Development, the Institutions, and the People of the Town of Pulaski, Tennessee.* Pulaski, TN: Private Printing, 1951.
GOOD87 "Giles County." *History of Tennessee.* ed. Weston A. Goodspeed et al., pp. 749-66, 846-76. Nashville: Goodspeed Publishing, 1887.
MCCA76 McCallum, James. *A Brief Sketch of the Settlement and Early History of Giles County, Tennessee.* Reprint of 1876 edition, Pulaski, TN: Pulaski Citizen, 1928 (reprinted 1983 by Southern Historical Press, Inc., Easley, SC).
PARK53 Parker, Elizabeth C. "History of Giles County, Tennessee." Murfreesboro, TN: Master's Thesis, Middle Tennessee State University, 1953.
SOLO76 Solomon, James. *Times from Giles County.* TN: Private printing, 1976.

GRAINGER COUNTY

GOOD87 "Grainger County." *History of Tennessee,* East Tennessee Edition, ed. Weston A. Goodspeed et al., pp. 853-56, 1152-60. Nashville: Goodspeed Publishing, 1887.
HOLT76 Holt, W.E. *Grainger County: 1796-1976.* TN: Grainger County Bicentennial Committee, 1976.

GREENE COUNTY

ALLE99 Allen, Charles W. *Historic Greenville, Tennessee. A City Among the Mountains.* New York: Moss, 1899.
GOOD87 "Greene County." *History of Tennessee,* East Tennessee Edition. ed. Weston A. Goodspeed et al., pp. 881-90, 1239-61. Nashville: Goodspeed Publishing, 1887.

GRUNDY COUNTY

NICH82 Nicholson, James L. *Grundy County.* Tennessee History Series, Memphis: Memphis State University Press, 1982.

HAMBLEN COUNTY

GOOD87 "Hamblen County." *History of Tennessee,* East Tennessee Edition, ed. Weston A. Goodspeed et al., pp. 868-71, 1200-16. Nashville: Goodspeed Publishing, 1887.
HCCC70 Hamblen County Centennial Celebration. *Historic Hamblen: 1870-1970.* Morristown, TN: Morrison Printing Co., 1970.

HAMILTON COUNTY

ARMS31 Armstrong, Zella. *The History of Hamilton County and Chattanooga, TN.* Chattanooga: The Lookout Publishing Co., 1931. Vol.1
GOOD87 "Hamilton County." *History of Tennessee,* East Tennessee Edition, ed. Weston A. Goodspeed et al., pp. 932-38. Nashville: Goodspeed Publishing, 1887.
LIVI81 Livingood, James W. *A History of Hamilton County.* Memphis: Memphis State University Press, 1981.
LIVI81 Livingood, James W. *Hamilton County.* Tennessee County History Series, Memphis: Memphis State University Press, 1981.
SHEP13 Shepherd, Lewis. "A Historical Sketch of the Courthouses of Hamilton County."

HANCOCK COUNTY

OOD87 "Hancock County." *History of Tennessee,* East Tennessee Edition, ed. Weston A. Goodspeed et al., pp. 871-72, 1216-25. Nashville: Goodspeed Publishing, 1887.
HCHG89 Hancock County Historical and Geneaological Society. *Hancock County, TN. and its People.* Salem, WV: Walsworth Publishing Co., 1989.

HARDEMAN COUNTY

CLIF30 Clift, Warner W. "Early History of Hardeman County, Tennessee. Nashville: Master's Thesis, George Peabody College, 1930.
GOOD87 "Hardeman County." *History of Tennessee.* ed. Weston A. Goodspeed et al., pp. 818-40, 887-963. Nashville: Goodspeed Publishing, 1887.
HCHC79 Hardeman County Historical Commission. *Hardeman County Historical Sketches.* Paducah, KY: Taylor Publishing Co., 1979.

HARDIN COUNTY

BRAZ1885 Brazelton, B.G. *A History of Hardin County, Tennessee.* Nashville: Cumberland Presbyterian Publishing House, 1885.
GOOD87 "Hardin County." *History of Tennessee.* ed. Weston A. Goodspeed et al., pp. 829-41, 894-908. Nashville: Goodspeed Publishing, 1887.
HAYS86 Hays, Tony. *From Forest to Farm: Hardin County History to 1860.* Kitchen Table Press, 1986.
HCHQ82 Williams, Henry E. and Grace Patterson. "The Courthouses of Hardin County, Tennessee," *Hardin County Historical Quarterly*, Vol. 1, No. 1, July-September 1982, p. 3-7.

HAWKINS COUNTY

GOOD87 "Hawkins County." *History of Tennessee,* East Tennessee Edition, ed. Weston A. Goodspeed et al., pp. 873-80, 1225-39. Nashville: Goodspeed Publishing, 1887.
HCBC76 Hawkins County Bicentennial Committee. *Hawkins County Picture Album.* East Tennessee Printing, 1976.

ROGA53   Rogan, James W. *Hawkins County*. Published in the Rogersville Review Dec. 19, 1889 to Nov. 27, 1990 (reprinted in same May 14, 1953 to August 13, 1953).

ROGA89   Rogan, James W. *Historical Sketches of Hawkins County*. Rogersville, TN: Hawkins County Geneaological & Historical Society, 1989.

HAYWOOD COUNTY

BHCH89   Brownsville-Haywood County Historical Society. *History of Haywood County, Tennessee*. Marceline. MO: Walsworth Publishing,, 1989.

GOOD87   "Haywood County." *History of Tennessee*. ed. Weston A. Goodspeed et al., pp. 818-29, 921-47. Nashville: Goodspeed Publishing, 1887.

HAYW39   *Haywood County Historical Records Survey*. Work's Progress Administration, 1939.

WPAS39   Historical Records Survey, Tennessee. *Inventory of the County Archives of Tennessee: Haywood County*. Nashville: The Survey, WPA, 1939.

HENDERSON COUNTY

BOLE22   Bolen, H.J. *Henderson County's History*. Murfreesboro, TN: *Home Journal*, 1922.

GOOD87   "Henderson County." *History of Tennessee*. ed. Weston A. Goodspeed et al., pp. 797-806, 841-62. Nashville: Goodspeed Publishing, 1887.

POWE30   Powers, Auburn. *History of Henderson County*. TN: Private Printing, 1930.

STEW79   Stewart, G. Tillman. *Henderson County*. Tennessee County History Series. Memphis: Memphis State University Press, 1979.

HENRY COUNTY

GREE00   Greene, W.P. *The City of Paris and Henry County, Tennessee, Historical, Descriptive, and Biographical*. Paris, TN: Paris Publishers, 1900.

GOOD87   "Henry County." *History of Tennessee*. ed. Weston A. Goodspeed et al., pp. 813-32, 888-935. Nashville: Goodspeed Publishing, 1887.

INMA76   Inman, W.O. *Pen Sketches: An Historical Pen Sketch of Henry County, Tennessee*. Paris, TN: The Guild Bindery Press, 1976.

JOHN58   Johnson, E. McLeod. *A History of Henry County, Tennessee, Vol l*. TN: Unpublished Typescript, 1958.

VAND66   Van Dyke, Roger Raymond. "A History of Henry County, Tennessee Through 1865." Knoxville: Master's Thesis, University of Tennessee, 1966.

VAND87   Van Dyke, Roger Raymond. *Antebellum Henry County*. Paris, TN: The Guild Bindery Press, 1987.

HICKMAN COUNTY

GOOD87   "Hickman County." *History of Tennessee*. ed. Weston A. Goodspeed et al., pp. 788-801,910-23. Nashville: Goodspeed Publishing, 1887.

HICK57   *Hickman County Sesquicentennial*. Columbia, TN: Columbia Printing Co., 1957.

SPEN00   Spence, Jerome D. and David L. Spence. *History of Hickman County, Tennessee*. Nashville: Gospel Advocate Publishing Co., 1900 (reprinted 1971 by Terry Durham).

HOUSTON COUNTY

GOOD87   "Houston County." *History of Tennessee*. ed. Weston A. Goodspeed et al., pp. 974-98, 1388-1402. Nashville: Goodspeed Publishing, 1887.

MCCL66   McClain, Iris Hopkins. *A History of Houston County, Tennessee*. TN: Private Printing, 1967.

HUMPHREYS COUNTY

GARR63   Garrett, Jill K. *A History of Humphreys County*. TN: Private Printing, 1963.

GOOD87   "Humphreys County." *History of Tennessee*. ed. Weston A. Goodspeed et al., pp. 868-94, 1205-88. Nashville: Goodspeed Publishing, 1887.

WHIT79   Whitfield, Margaret (editor). *Humphreys County Heritage*. Dallas: Humprhreys County Historical Society, 1979.

JACKSON COUNTY

DRAP29   Draper, R.C. "Early History of Jackson County, Tennessee." Gainesboro, TN: *Jackson County Sentinel*, 1928-29 (published as a series of newspaper articles).

JACK38   *Jackson County Historical Records Project*. Work's Progress Administration, 1938.

TAYS89   Tayse, Moldon Jenkins. *Jackson County, Tennessee*. Private printing, 1989.

JAMES COUNTY

DONN83   Donnelly, Polly W., Ed. James County. Collegedale, TN: Collegedale Press, 1983.

GOOD87   "James County." *History of Tennessee*, East Tennessee Edition ed. Weston A. Goodspeed et al., pp. 797-98, 955-62. Nashville: Goodspeed Publishing, 1887.

OLDJ83   Old James County Chapter. *James County: A Lost County of Tennessee*. Collegedale, TN: East Tennessee Historical Society, 1983.

JEFFERSON COUNTY

BIBL91   Bible, Jean P. *Bent Twigs in Jefferson County*. Collegedale, TN: East Tennesse Printing Co., 1991.

BCJC76   Bicentennial Committee of Jefferson County. *Heritage Jefferson County*. Private printing, 1976.

GOOD87   "Jefferson County." *History of Tennessee*, East Tennessee Edition. ed. Weston A. Goodspeed et al., pp. 856-64, 1160-93. Nashville: Goodspeed Publishing, 1887.

JCHS86   Jefferson County High School. *Windows to the Past: A Structural History of Jefferson County*. Private Printing, 1986.

MUNC94   Muncy, Estle P. *People and Places of Jefferson County*. Rogersville, TN: East Tennesse Printing Co., 1994.

JOHNSON COUNTY

GOOD87   "Johnson County." *History of Tennessee*, East Tennessee Edition, ed. Weston A. Goodspeed et al., pp. 922-25, 1312-17. Nashville: Goodspeed Publishing, 1887.

JCHS85   Johnson County Historical Society. *History of Johnson County*. Marceline, MO: Walsworth Press, 1985.

KNOX COUNTY

CREE88   Creekmore, Betsey Beeler. *Knox County, Tennesseee: A History in Pictures*. Norfolk, VA: Donning Company Publishers, 1988.

GOOD87   "Knox County." *History of Tennessee*, East Tennessee Edition, ed. Weston A. Goodspeed et al., pp. 925-31. Nashville: Goodspeed Publishing, 1887.

GOOD88 "Knox County and Knoxville." *History of Tennessee, Knox County and Knoxville Edition,* ed. Weston A. Goodspeed et al., pp. 797-1072. Nashville: Goodspeed Publishing, 1887.

LAKE COUNTY

GOOD87 "Lake County." *History of Tennessee.* ed. Weston A. Goodspeed et al., pp. 852-57, 1073-87. Nashville: Goodspeed Publishing, 1887.

LCHS93 Lake County Historical Society. *Lake County, Tennessee.* Paducah, KY: Turner Publishing Co., 1993.

LAUDERDALE COUNTY

GOOD87 "Lauderdale County." *History of Tennessee.* ed. Weston A. Goodspeed et al., pp. 797-807, 842-85. Nashville: Goodspeed Publishing, 1887.

MCKInd McKinney, Colin P. "History of Lauderdale County." Unpublished typescript, n.d. (Microfilm, TSLA).

PETE57 Peters, Kate Johnson (editor). *Lauderdale County from Earliest Times.* Jackson, TN: Sugar Hill Lauderdale County Library, 1957.

LAWRENCE COUNTY

CARP86 Carpenter, Viola Hagan and Marymaud Killen Carter. *Our Hometown: Lawrenceburg, TN.* Lawrenceburg, TN: Lino-Litho Printers, 1986.

COLE94 Cole, Estha. *Places in Lawrence County, Tennessee, Then and Now.* Private printing, 1994.

GOOD87 "Lawrence County." *History of Tennessee.* ed. Weston A. Goodspeed et al., pp. 749-63, 807-49. Nashville: Goodspeed Publishing, 1887.

MORR68 Morrison, John F. "A Brief History of Lawrence County, Tennessee." Lawrenceburg, TN: Unpublished typescript, 1968.

LEWIS COUNTY

GOOD87 "Lewis County." *History of Tennessee.* ed. Weston A. Goodspeed et al., pp. 801-07, 923-24. Nashville: Goodspeed Publishing, 1887.

LINCOLN COUNTY

DICK77 Dickey, Elaine Owens. *Lincoln County: A Tribute to Our Past.* Fayetteville, TN: Dickey Publications, 1977.

GOOD87 "Lincoln County." *History of Tennessee.* ed. Weston A. Goodspeed et al., pp. 767-84, 876-924. Nashville: Goodspeed Publishing, 1887.

MARS89 Marsh, Timothy R. and Helen C. (Editors). *First County Court Minutes, Lincoln County, TN.* Easley, SC: Southern Historical Press, Inc., 1989.

LOUDON COUNTY

DART62 Daughters of the American Revolution, Tennessee. *Beloved Landmarks of Loudon County, Tennessee.* Loudon, TN: Hiwassee Chapter, DAR, 1962.

GOOD87 "Loudon County." *History of Tennessee,* East Tennessee Edition ed. Weston A. Goodspeed et al., pp. 825-28, 1081-88. Nashville: Goodspeed Publishing, 1887.

IMAG86 Images Publications. *Loudon County: We Call It Home.* Loudon, TN: Images Publications, 1986.

WPAS41 Historical Records Survey, Tennessee. *Inventory of the County Archives of Tennessee, Loudon County.* Nashville: The Survey, WPA, 1941.

MACON COUNTY

BLAN86 Blankenship, Harold G. *History of Macon County, Tennessee.* Tompkinsville, KY: Monroe County Press, 1986.

GOOD87 "Macon County." *History of Tennessee.* ed. Weston A. Goodspeed et al., pp. 843-41, 971-88. Nashville: Goodspeed Publishing, 1887.

MADISON COUNTY

GOOD87 "Madison County." *History of Tennessee.* ed. Weston A. Goodspeed et al., pp. 797-917. Nashville: Goodspeed Publishing, 1887.

WILL46 Williams, Emma May. *Historic Madison: The Story of Jackson and Madison County Tennessee.* Jackson, TN: Madison County Historical Society, 1946.

MARION COUNTY

LINK53 Link, Gertrude B. "A History of Marion County." Murfreesboro, TN: Master's Thesis, Middle Tennessee State University, 1953.

MARI90 Marion County Historical Society. *The Story of Marion County: Its People and Places.* Dallas: Curtis Media Corp. 1990.

MARSHALL COUNTY

GOOD87 "Marshall County." *History of Tennessee.* ed. Weston A. Goodspeed et al., pp. 884-903, 1190-1232. Nashville: Goodspeed Publishing, 1887.

MARS86 Marshall County Historical Society. *Marshall County, Tennessee: A Sesquicentennial History.* Marceline, MO: Walsworth Press, 1986.

WRIG63 Wright, Mitchel. *A History of Marshall County, Tennessee.* Franklin, TN: Private Printing, 1963.

MAURY COUNTY

GARR86 Garrett, Jill K. *Hither and Yon: The Best of the Writings of Jill K. Garrett.* Columbia, TN: Maury Country Homecoming '86 Committee, 1986.

GOOD87 "Maury County." *History of Tennessee.* ed. Weston A. Goodspeed et al., pp. 749-87, 904-65. Nashville: Goodspeed Publishing, 1887.

SMIT69 Smith, Frank H. *Frank H. Smith's History of Maury County, Tennessee.* Columbia, TN: Maury County Historical Society, 1969.

TURN55 Turner, William B. *History of Maury County, Tennessee.* Nashville: Parthenon Press, 1955.

MCMINN COUNTY

BYRU84 Byrum, C. Stephen. *McMinn County.* Tennessee County History Series, Memphis: Memphis State University Press, 1984.

GOOD87 "McMinn County." *History of Tennessee,* East Tennessee Edition, ed. Weston A. Goodspeed et al., pp. 811-15, 1012-32. Nashville: Goodspeed Publishing, 1887.

WOMA60 Womak, John W. *McMinnville, Tennessee: 1818-1960.* McMinnville, TN: Standard Publish Co., 1960.

MCNAIRY COUNTY

ADAM52 Adams, J. Louis. *Old Purdy: The History of the first County Seat of McNairy County, Tennessee.* Jackson, TN: McCowat-Mercer Press, 1952.

GOOD87 "McNairy County." *History of Tennessee.* ed. Weston A. Goodspeed et al., pp. 819-28, 870-80. Nashville: Goodspeed Publishing, 1887.

WHIT73 Whitlow, Charles and Myrlee Wright. *150 Years of Growth & Progress in McNairy County, Vol. 1.* Jackson, TN: McCowat-Mercer Press, 1973.

WRIG68 Wright, Gen. Marcus J. *Reminiscences of the Early Settlement and Early Settlers of McNairy County, Tennessee.* (Reprint of 1882 edition) Memphis: Tri-State Printing & Binding, 1968.

MEIGS COUNTY

LILL75 Lillard, Stewart. *Meigs County, Tennessee: A Documented Account of Its European Settlement and Growth.* Sewanee, TN: University Press, 1975.

GOOD87 "Meigs County." *History of Tennessee,* East Tennessee Edition, ed. Weston A. Goodspeed et al., pp. 815-17, 1032-36. Nashville: Goodspeed Publishing, 1887.

MONROE COUNTY

GOOD87 "Monroe County." *History of Tennessee,* East Tennessee Edition, ed. Weston A. Goodspeed et al., pp. 807-11, 994-1012. Nashville: Goodspeed Publishing, 1887.

SAND82 Sands, Sarah G. Cox. *History of Monroe County, Tennessee.* Baltimore: Gateway Press, 1982.

MONTGOMERY COUNTY

BEAC64 Beach, Ursula S. *Along the Warioto, A History of Montgomery County, Tennessee.* Nashville: McQuiddy Press, 1964.

BEAC88 Beach, Ursula S. *Montgomery County.* Tennessee County History Series, Memphis: Memphis State University Press, 1988.

GOOD87 "Montgomery County." *History of Tennessee.* ed. Weston A. Goodspeed et al., pp. 749-827, 999-1124. Nashville: Goodspeed Publishing, 1887.

THTR95 *The National Trade Review (Clarksville, TN Edition).* Evansville, IN: Keller Printing Co., 1895.

MOORE COUNTY

GOOD87 "Moore County." *History of Tennessee.* ed. Weston A. Goodspeed et al., pp. 804-19, 924-34. Nashville: Goodspeed Publishing, 1887.

MORGAN COUNTY

DICK87 Dickson, W. Calvin. *Morgan County.* Tennessee County History Series, Memphis: Memphis State University Press, 1987.

FREY71 Freytag, Ethel, and Glena K. Ott. *A History of Morgan County, Tennessee.* Wartburg, TN: Specialty, 1971.

GOOD87 "Morgan County." *History of Tennessee,* East Tennessee Edition, ed. Weston A. Goodspeed et al., pp. 841-43, 1123-25. Nashville: Goodspeed Publishing, 1887.

OBION COUNTY

GOOD87 "Obion County." *History of Tennessee.* ed. Weston A. Goodspeed et al., pp. 816-31, 932-84. Nashville: Goodspeed Publishing, 1887.

MARS41 Marshall, E.H. *History of Obion County.* Union City, TN: Daily Messenger, 1941.

OCHS81 Obion County Historical Society. *Obion County History.* Dallas: Taylor Publishing Co., 1981.

OVERTON COUNTY

ELDR76 Eldridge, Robert L. and Mary. *Bicentennial Echoes of the History of Overton County, Tennessee.* Livingston, TN: Enterprise Printing Co., 1976.

KNIG72 Knight, George Allen. *Our Wonderful Overton County Heritage.* Privately published, 1972.

PERRY COUNTY

GOOD87 "Perry County." *History of Tennessee.* ed. Weston A. Goodspeed et al., pp. 777-88, 889-909. Nashville: Goodspeed Publishing, 1887.

PICKETT COUNTY

HUDD73 Huddleston, Tim. *History of Pickett County.* Collegedale, TN: The College Press, 1973.

PCBC91 Pickett County Book Committee. *History and Geneaolgy of Families in Pickett County.* 1991.

POLK COUNTY

BARC75 Barclay, R.E. *The Copper Basin - 18890 to 1968.* Knoxville: Cole Printing, 1975.

GOOD87 "Polk County." *History of Tennessee,* East Tennessee Edition ed. Weston A. Goodspeed et al., pp. 804-07, 987-94. Nashville: Goodspeed Publishing, 1887.

PUTNAM COUNTY

DELO79 DeLozier, Mary Jean. *Putnam County, Tennessee 1850-1970.* Nashville: Putnam County (pub.) 1979.

MCCL25 McClain, Walter S. *A History of Putnam County.* Cookville, TN: Quimby Dyer & Co. 1925.

RHEA COUNTY

BROY91 Broyles, Bettye J. (compiler). *History of Rhea County, Tennessee.* Collegedale, TN: Rhea County Historical and Geneaological Society, 1991.

GOOD87 "Rhea County." *History of Tennessee,* East Tennessee Edition, ed. Weston A. Goodspeed et al., pp. 817-21, 1046-71. Nashville: Goodspeed Publishing, 1887.

ROANE COUNTY

GOOD87 "Roane County." *History of Tennessee,* East Tennessee Edition ed. Weston A. Goodspeed et al., pp. 821-25, 1072-81. Nashville: Goodspeed Publishing, 1887.

PICK71 Pickel, Eugene. "A History of Roane County to 1860." Knoxville: Master's Thesis, University of Tennessee, 1971.

WELL27 Wells, Emma H.M. *The History of Roane County, Tennessee, 1801-1870.* Chattanooga: Lookout Publishing, 1927.

WILL82 Williams, Frank, V. III. *Pictures of the Past.* Kingston, TN: Roane County Heritage Commission, 1982.

ROBERTSON COUNTY

BRUN61 Brunson, Suzanne. "Can Springfield's Tower Stay Up Much Longer?" *Nashville Banner,* October 11, 1961.

GOOD87 "Robertson County." *History of Tennessee.* ed. Weston A. Goodspeed et al., pp. 827-67, 1124-1205. Nashville: Goodspeed Publishing, 1887.

HOLM71 Holman, Catherine and Jean Durrett. *Historic Robertson County: Places and Personalities.* Privately published, undated (ca1971).

TNHC Tennessee Historical Commission. National Register Nomination for the Robertson County Courthouse.

RUTHERFORD COUNTY

GOOD87 "Rutherford County." *History of Tennessee.* ed. Weston A. Goodspeed et al., pp. 810-40, 1019-76. Nashville: Goodspeed Publishing, 1887.

PITT84 Pittard, Mabel. *Rutherford County.* Tennessee County History Series, Memphis: Memphis State University Press, 1984.

RCBC76 Rutherford County Bicentennial Commission. *Griffith.* Murfreesboro, TN: Private Printing, 1976.

SIMS47 Sims, Carlton C. (editor). *A History of Rutherford County.* Murfreesboro, TN.: Private Printing, 1947.

TUCK78 Burney Tucker & Associates. *Master Plan for the Preservation and Restoration of the Rutherford County Courthouse.* Nashville, TN: Private Printing, 1978.

WPAS38 Historical Records Survey, Tennessee. *Inventory of the County Archives of Tennessee: Rutherford County.* Nashville: The Survey, WPA, 1938.

SCOTT COUNTY

SAND58 Sanderson, Esther Sharp. *County Scott & Its Mountain Folk.* Nashville: Williams Printing Co., 1958.

SAND74 Sanderson, Esther Sharp. *Scott County Gem of the Cumberlands.* Huntsville, TN.: Esther Sharp Sanderson, 1974.

SMIT85 Smith, H. Clay. *Dusty Bits of the Forgotten Past (Scott County).* Nashville: Scott County Historical Society, 1985.

SEQUATCHIE COUNTY

CAMP84 Camp, Henry R. *Sequatchie County.* Tennessee County History Series, Memphis: Memphis State University Press, 1984.

LAYN69 Layne, Ora. *Sequatchie County: History and Development.* Dunlap, TN: Private Printing, 1969.

RAUL74 Raulston, J. Leonard and James W. Livingood. *Sequatchie: A Story of the Southern Cumberlands.* Knoxville: University of Tennessee Press, 1974.

SEVIER COUNTY

MATT60 Matthews, Fred D. *History of Sevier County.* Knoxville: Master, c. 1950. Rev. ed., Knoxville: 1960.

GOOD87 "Sevier County." *History of Tennessee,* East Tennessee Edition, ed. Weston A. Goodspeed et al., pp. 834-37, 1096-1104. Nashville: Goodspeed Publishing, 1887.

SCHB94 Sevier COunty Heritage Book Committee. *Sevier County, Tennessee and Its Heritage.* Waynesville, NC: Walsworth Publishing Co., 1994.

SHELBY COUNTY

CHAN53 Chandler, Walter. "The Court Houses of Shelby County." *WTHSP* vol.. 7 (1953), pp. 72-78.

COPP76 Coppeck, Paul R. *Memphis Sketches.* Memphis: Friends of Memphis & Shelby Co. Libraries, 1976.

DAVI72 Davis, James D. *History of Memphis. The History of the City of Memphis.* Memphis: Hite, Crumpton & Killy, 1832; rpt. West Tennessee Historical Society, 1972.

KEAT89 Keating, John M. *History of the City of Memphis and Shelby County, Tennessee, with Illustrations and Biographical Sketches of Some of Its Prominent Citizens.* Syracuse, NY: D. Mason, 1888, 1889.

GOOD87 "Shelby County." *History of Tennessee.* ed. Weston A. Goodspeed et al., pp. 797-1063. Nashville: Goodspeed Publishing, 1887.

SMITH COUNTY

BOWEnd Bowen, John W. *Smith County History.* N.p., n.d., TSLA.

GOOD87 "Smith County." *History of Tennessee.* ed. Weston A. Goodspeed et al., pp. 821-34, 929-71. Nashville: Goodspeed Publishing, 1887.

MAGG86 Maggart, Sue W. and Nina R. Sutton (editors). *The History of Smith County, TN.* Dallas: Curtis Media Corp. and Smith County Homecoming '86 Heritage Committee, 1986.

SMIT87 Smith County Homecoming '86 Heritage Committee. The History of Smith County. Dallas: Curtis Media Corp., 1987.

STEWART COUNTY

BRAN44 Brandon, Helen Gould. *A History of Stewart County, TN.* Knoxville: Master of Arts Thesis, University of Tennessee, 1944.

GOOD87 "Stewart County." *History of Tennessee.* ed. Weston A. Goodspeed et al., pp. 894-920, 1289-1329. Nashville: Goodspeed Publishing, 1887.

MCCL65 McClain, Iris Hopkins. *A History of Stewart County, TN.* Columbia, TN: Private Printing, 1965.

SCHS80 Stewart County Heritage Society. *Stewart County Heritage.* Dover, TN: Stewart County Heritage Society, 1980.

SULLIVAN COUNTY

GOOD87 "Sullivan County." *History of Tennessee,* East Tennessee Edition, ed. Weston A. Goodspeed et al., pp. 912-21, 1300-1312. Nashville: Goodspeed Publishing, 1887.

HTGS93 Hosten Territory Geneaological Society. *Families and History of Sullivan County, Tennessee.* Waynesville, NC: Walsworth Publishing Co., 1993.

SPOD76 Spoden, Muriel C. (editor). *Historic Sites of Sullivan County.* Kingsport, TN.: Sullivan County Court/Kingsport Press, 1976.

TAYL09 Taylor, Oliver. *Historic Sullivan.* Bristol, TN: The King Printing Co., 1909.

WPAS40 Historical Records Survey. *Inventory of the County Archives of Tennessee: Sullivan County.* Nashville: The Survey, WPA, 1940.

SUMNER COUNTY

DURH72 Durham, Walter T. *Old Sumner: A History of Sumner County, TN. from 1805 to 1861.* Nashville: Sumner County Public Library Board, 1972.

DURH86 Durham, Walter T. and James W. Thomas. *A Pictorial History of Sumner County, TN. 1786-1986.* Nashville: Sumner County Historical Society, 1986.

GOOD87 "Sumner County." *History of Tennessee.* ed. Weston A. Goodspeed et al., pp. 797-821, 848-929. Nashville: Goodspeed Publishing, 1887.

TIPTON COUNTY

BEAS81 Beasley, Gaylon Neil. *True Tales of Tipton, Historical Accounts of Tipton County*. Nashville: Tipton County Historical Society, 1981.

GOOD87 "Tipton County." *History of Tennessee*. ed. Weston A. Goodspeed et al., pp. 808-818, 885-921. Nashville: Goodspeed Publishing, 1887.

WPAS41 Historical Records Survey, Tennessee. *Inventory of the County Archives of Tennessee: Tipton County*. Nashville: The Survey, WPA, 1941.

TROUSDALE COUNTY

GOOD87 "Trousdale County." *History of Tennessee*. ed. Weston A. Goodspeed et al., pp. 841-48, 988-91. Nashville: Goodspeed Publishing, 1887.

MCMU70 McMurtry, J.C. *History of Trousdale County*. Vidette Printing Co., 1970.

TROU85 Trousdale County Historical Society. *A Pictorial Collection of Trousdale County's Past*. Hartsville, TN: private printing, 1985.

UNICOI COUNTY

GOOD87 "Unicoi County." *History of Tennessee*, East Tennessee Edition ed. Weston A. Goodspeed et al., pp. 904-06, 1287-89. Nashville: Goodspeed Publishing, 1887.

HELT86 Helton, William W. *Around Home in Unicoi County*. Johnson City, TN: Overmountain Press, 1986.

UNION COUNTY

GOOD87 "Union County." *History of Tennessee*, East Tennessee Edition, ed. Weston A. Goodspeed et al., pp. 850-52, 1146-52. Nashville: Goodspeed Publishing, 1887.

GRAV78 Graves, Kathleen George and Winnie Palmer McDonald. *Our Union County Heritage*. TN: Joston's, 1978.

PAGE86 Page, Bonnie M. *Union County (Its Cities, Towns and Points of Interest)*. Clinton, TN: Clinton Courier-News, 1986.

THAR85 Tharpe, William G. and Norman L. Collins (editors). *From Hearth and Hoe: Union County, Tennessee 1910-1940*. TN:

VAN BUREN COUNTY

MEDL87 Medley, Landon Daryle. *The History of Van Buren County, TN*. Salem, WV: Don Mills, Inc., 1987.

WARREN COUNTY

DILL81 James A. Dillon. "Once Upon A Time," *Warren County News*, December 29, 1981.

DILL83 James A. Dillon. "Once Upon A Time," *Southern Standard*, May 27, 1983.

GOOD87 "Warren County." *History of Tennessee*. ed. Weston A. Goodspeed et al., pp. 812-27, 884-921. Nashville: Goodspeed Publishing, 1887.

HALE30 Hale, Will T. *Early History of Warren County*. McMinneville, TN: Standard Printing Co., 1930

WISE95 Wiseman, Eugene M. *The Warren County Story*. Franklin, NC: Genealogy Publishing Services, 1995.

WOMA60 Womack, John W. *McMinnville At A Milestone*. McMinnville, TN: Standard Publishing Co., 1960.

WASHINGTON COUNTY

GOOD87 "Washington County." *History of Tennessee*, East Tennessee Edition, ed. Weston A. Goodspeed et al., pp. 891-904, 1262-86. Nashville: Goodspeed Publishing, 1887.

WATA88 Watauga Association of Genealogists. *History of Washington Co., TN*. Salem, WV: Walsworth Press, 1988.

WAYNE COUNTY

GOOD87 "Wayne County." *History of Tennessee*. ed. Weston A. Goodspeed et al., pp. 763-77, 849-89. Nashville: Goodspeed Publishing, 1887.

WCHS Wayne County Historical Society. ??

WEAKLEY COUNTY

GOOD87 "Weakley County." *History of Tennessee*. ed. Weston A. Goodspeed et al., pp. 831-42, 985-1024. Nashville: Goodspeed Publishing, 1887.

VAUG83 Vaughan, Virginia C. *Weakley County*. Tennessee County History Series. Memphis: Memphis State University Press, 1983.

WHITE COUNTY

GOOD87 "White County." *History of Tennessee*. ed. Weston A. Goodspeed et al., pp. 797-812, 860-84. Nashville: Goodspeed Publishing, 1887.

LEON84 Leonard, Charles. *Pictorial History of Sparta - White County, Tennessee*. Cookville, TN: First National Bank of Sparta, 1984.

ROGE72 Rogers, E.G. *Memorable Historical Accounts of White County and Area*. Collegedale, TN: The College Press, 1972.

SEAL35 Seals, Monroe. *History of White County*. N.p., 1935.

WILLIAMSON COUNTY

BOWM71 Bowman, Virginia McDaniel. *Historic Williamson County*. Nashville: Blue & Gray Press, 1971.

GOOD87 "Williamson County." *History of Tennessee*. ed. Weston A. Goodspeed et al., pp. 787-810, 965-1019. Nashville: Goodspeed Publishing, 1887.

WILSON COUNTY

BURN83 Burns, Frank. *Wilson County*. Tennessee County History Series, Memphis: Memphis State University Press, 1983.

GOOD87 "Wilson County." *History of Tennessee*. ed. Weston A. Goodspeed et al., pp. 840-61, 1077-1125. Nashville: Goodspeed Publishing, 1887.

MERR61 Merritt, DIxon (Editor, senior contributor). *The History of Wilson County: Its Land and Its Life*. Nashville: Benson Printing Co., 1961.

WPAS38 Historical Records Survey, Tennessee. *Inventory of the County Archives of Tennessee: Wilson County*. Nashville: The Survey, WPA, 1938.

PHOTOGRAPHIC TECHNICAL DATA

Cameras	Linhof Master Technika with Linhof 150mm
	Ebony 4 x 5
	Wisner Convertible Classic 5 x 7
	Deardorf 8 x 10
Meters	Sekonic avg/1° Sekonic 1°/3°
Tripod	Topcon surveyors heavy duty with Gitzo V head
Lenses	Schneider 90mm f/5.6 Super Angulon.
	Schneider 150mm f/5.6 Symmar - S.
	Schneider 210mm f/5.6 Symmar - S.
	Schneider 270mm f/8
	Schneider 355 mm f/9 G-Claron.
	Aerojet Delft 6" f/2.8 type I Hycon P/N in Copal 3-S.
	aus Jena DDR f/4.5 360mm Giant Tessar.
Film	Kodak Sheet Tri-X 4 x 5, 5 x 7 & 8 x 10
Developer	(film) Kodak HC110 Dil B (in trays)
Paper	Kodak ELITE Grades 2, 3 & 4
Developer	(paper) Kodak Dektol (working solution 1-2)
Enlarger	Omega D2 4 x 5 with diachroic head
Lens	Schneider 150mm Componon 4

Michael Emrick, AIA

Michael Emrick is a native of Indiana and has been a Tennessee resident since 1978. He is one of Tennessee's leading preservation architects and maintains an architectural/preservation practice in Tennessee and the Southeast as well as nation-wide. His past publications have included the *Handbook of Maintenance Techniques* for The Strand Historic District in Galveston, historic preservation manuals and design guidelines for Cheraw, SC and Gainesboro, TN, Fort McPherson, Fort Benning and the Naval Supply Corps School (Georgia); the award-winning Master Plan for the Rugby Colony (Tennessee), and four studies on historic structures in the Kingdom of Saudi Arabia.

Michael's past restoration projects have included two Tennessee courthouses--the old Roane County and Rutherford County courthouses as well as several state historic structures, including the Tennessee State Capitol in Nashville, the James K. Polk Home in Columbia, the Sam Davis Home in Smyrna, Blount Mansion and the Old City Hall in Knoxville, Cragfont in Gallatin, Wynnewood in Castilian Springs, the Carter House in Franklin, and Oaklands Mansion in Murfreesboro. He has also served on the Mansion Restoration Committee at The Hermitage and is on the Board of Directors of Historic Nashville, Inc.

In recognition of his preservation work, Michael has received several awards from the Metro Historical Commission, Tennessee Historical Commission, AIA/Tennessee, AIA/Gulf States, and *Progressive Architecture* magazine.

In addition to articles for the *Tennessee Architect* and its successor *ArchitectureSouth,* Michael's publications include an article on the evolution of Blount Mansion for the Tennessee Historical Society *Quarterly* and an annotated map of Davidson County historical sites for Historic Nashville, Inc.

When not working on historic building projects for clients, Michael enjoys reading science fiction and historical novels and mysteries, collecting stamps, and occasional travel and scuba diving. When bored, he continues to plug away on the renovation of his home in Nashville's Germantown historic district.

With the publication of *Tennessee Courthouses*, Michael provides an historical perspective on the design of county courthouses in the Tennessee, incorporating over 200 historical photographs, sketches, and postcard views showing earlier views of the current and past courthouses in Tennessee's 95 counties.

John W. Carpenter

John W. Carpenter is a native of London, Kentucky, born July 8, 1927, and the only son of the late W. S. and Bess Carpenter. After graduation from high school he did a two-year hitch in the army as a drill sergeant. The next six years were spent at the University of Kentucky where he received degrees in Mechanical and Civil Engineering. After graduation he went to work for Combustion Engineering Inc., an international manufacturer of steam boilers for utility plants. Then the travel began; the next 11 years saw him in 30 states and 12 countries. In 1964 he returned to London to join his father's business, and remained there until his retirement in 1990.

Photography (35mm) has been a serious hobby since high school, but he moved into large format in 1984. Color photography was abandoned in 1988 for serious black and white work. He has worked with Sexton, Gaglianni and Wisner; refining skills and techniques.

Carpenter describes himself as being hobby-poor. In addition to photography, he has become a serious MEL instrument pilot, professional tennis instructor, amateur astronomer, a telescope and mirror maker, competitive skeet and pistol shooter, archer, cabinet maker, snow skier, wine and champagne maker along with fishing and wing shooting. He is now working on a photographic documentary on the Daniel Boone National Forest. This will involve hiking, camping, ATVing and horseback riding over the next 4 or 5 years.

John W. Carpenter's Kentucky Courthouses became a reality in 1988 and in time for the Kentucky Bicentennial in 1992. He made the statement that "if I get my money back on the Kentucky book, I'll do a sequel for the Tennessee Bicentennial in 1996." So here it is, 1996, the bicentennial year, and here is the book: **John W. Carpenter's Tennessee Courthouses**. Carpenter ranks the publication of these two books, along with becoming an Eagle Scout, as his proudest accomplishments.

The art of whittling still lives in Clay County. These whittlers benches show lots of use!

Memories of the War Between the States abound in Western Tennessee as in Gibson County (above) and Weakley County (left).

The dilemma of Grundy County courthouse is shown in the shot (above). No wonder we couldn't find it! Below is the church used for court, and the trailer which was used for offices.

My favorite "motto" on all the statues we saw in Tennessee was made by Robert A. "Fats" Everett. "If a man don't want to work he hadn't ought to hire out." (above)

Sevier County's most famous celebrity "in bronze" in front of the beautiful Sevier courthouse.
MISS DOLLY PARTON

Feelings ran high in those days. I wonder if we have this kind of grit today? (above)

County maps in the terrazzo floor of McNairy (above right) and Lauderdale. (right)

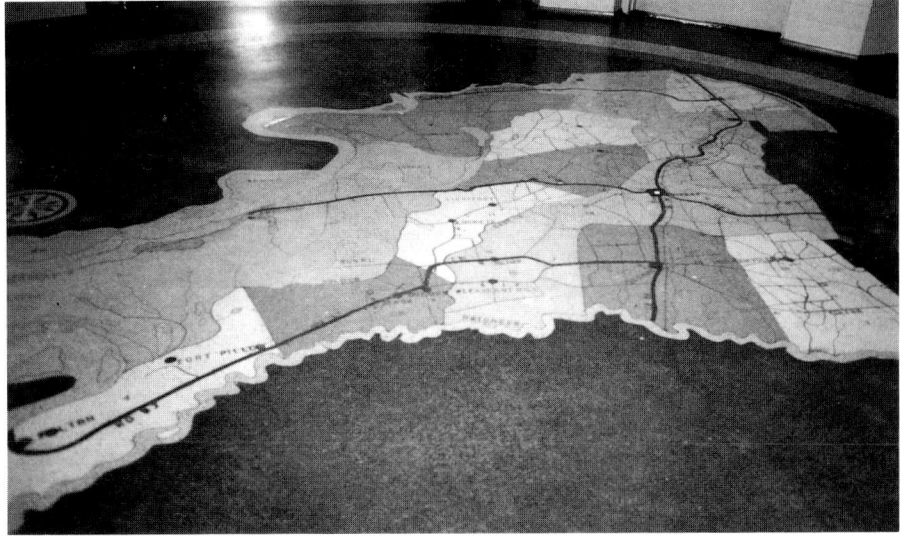

One of the focal points of any community is the courthouse — the place where so much of Kentucky's rich and fascinating history has been written. We Kentuckians have a natural interest in our past, and John Carpenter's *Kentucky Courthouses* takes you on an unusual and fascinating trip, stopping at every courthouse in existence in the Commonwealth.

As a Kentuckian, a student of history, or a lover of photography, you will enjoy this journey. I also proudly commend John Carpenter for contributing his work to enhancing future generations' understanding and appreciation for this special place called home.

Martha Layne Collins
Governor
Commonwealth of Kentucky
1983-87

GOVERNOR WALLACE G. WILKINSON
CAPITOL
FRANKFORT, KENTUCKY 40601

July 15, 1988

Mr. John Carpenter
West Fifth Street
London, Kentucky 40741

Dear Mr. Carpenter,

    As I have travelled across Kentucky, I've had the opportunity to visit every courthouse in this beautiful Commonwealth. Only when you have seen them all, can you get a true appreciation for the history represented by these unique and individual landmarks.

    In most of our counties, the courthouse is the heart of the community. Each is different from the other; distinctive in its architecture and its history.

    Congratulations on compiling a magnificent tribute to Kentucky's courthouses. For the vast majority of Kentuckians, who will never have the opportunity to visit each of these magnificent structures, your book is the next best thing to being there.

Sincerely,

Wallace G. Wilkinson

The Kentucky Bicentennial Commission

July 29, 1988

John W. Carpenter
London Bucket Company, Inc.
Post Office Box 370
London, Kentucky 40741

Dear Mr. Carpenter:

I certainly enjoyed meeting with you Tuesday. Your pictorial history of Kentucky's Courthouses will be a significant addition to Kentucky's history and to its upcoming bicentennial.

As we discussed, Mr. Carpenter, perhaps the best avenue for you to follow would be to address the Kentucky Bicentennial Commission at their next quarterly meeting in Pikeville. At that meeting you may want to request the endorsement of the full commission. I will keep you informed of meeting details, time and location.

Again, thank you for the opportunity to review your proposal. If you have any questions, please do not hesitate to call me.

Sincerely,

Daniel G. Carey

The Kentucky Bicentennial Commission
1792 - 1992

December 19, 1988

John W. Carpenter
711 West Fifth Street
London, Kentucky 40741

Dear Mr. Carpenter:

Thank you for sending me an embossed copy of <u>Kentucky Courthouses</u>. The photographs are wonderful and in many instances enhance the appearance of the buildings. Through your efforts I am more aware of the beauty as well as the importance of Kentucky courthouses. I must commend you on an excellent job.

A copy of the book was circulated at our Commission meeting last week. The members and state agency representatives had a chance to review the completed work. If their reactions evolve into purchases, I am sure you will sell many copies in the near future.

Once again I thank you for sending me a copy of <u>Kentucky Courthouses</u>. I and my coffee table are richer because of it.

Best regards and many thanks,

Sherry G. Sebastian
Administrative Assistant,
Kentucky Bicentennial Commission

The Kentucky Bicentennial Commission
1792 - 1992

December 19, 1988

Mr. John W. Carpenter
711 West Fifth Street
London, Kentucky 40741

Dear John:

    Thank you for sending me a copy of your <u>Kentucky Courthouses</u>. I have enjoyed reading about my own county courthouse in Jefferson County as well as the others in the state. I have also enjoyed looking at the beautiful photographs. I must say that before your book was published I never knew the beauty many of these buildings possessed. Now, it is quite clear why you chose to do a photographic study of them.

    I took the book to our Commission meeting last week. The members were impressed with the finished product and with the way in which the Commission's logo appeared. Everyone agreed the work was tastefully done and many members expressed interest in purchasing a copy for themselves.

    John, the Commission commends your efforts in providing an important piece of Kentucky history to those who yearn for it.

Best wishes and Happy Holidays,

Dave

David K. Karem
Chairman, Kentucky Bicentennial
  Commission

ss

BILL J. WRIGHT
CERTIFIED PETROLEUM GEOLOGIST
CPG # 987
101 PARK AVE., SUITE 665 ☐ OKLAHOMA CITY, OKLAHOMA 73102 ☐ (405) 232-5785

7 April 1989

Mr. John Carpenter
P.O. Box 804
London, Ky, 40741

Dear Mr. Carpenter,

Enclosed is my check # 3377 for $36.00. Please send me a copy of "Kentucky Courthouses".

I ran across this excellent book in Princeton, Ky while photographing courthouses.

I have personally photographed over 2400 courthouses in forty four states. I have corresponded with several publishers but have not received much encouragement.

Any advice you can offer about finding a publisher or self-publishing would be appreciated.

Sincerely,
Bill J. Wright

DANIEL L. DICKERSON

ATTORNEY & COUNSELOR AT LAW
7033 BURLINGTON PIKE
P.O. BOX 276
FLORENCE, KENTUCKY 41042-0276
(606) 283-2200

DANIEL L. DICKERSON   ALSO ADMITTED IN OHIO

April 10, 1989

Mr. John W. Carpenter
P.O. Box 804
London, Kentucky 40741

RE: Kentucky Courthouses

Dear Mr. Carpenter:

    I recently reviewed your book, Kentucky Courthouses, in Judge Sam Neace's Office in Boone County, Kentucky. I found the book to be extremely interesting and well written. Please forward a copy of the book to my office at your earliest convenience. My office will reimburse you for the cost of the book and any shipping expenses.

    Thanking you for your cooperation, I am,

                                         Sincerely,

                                         Daniel L. Dickerson

DLD/slh

LAW OFFICES OF

HOGG, CORNETT, & TURNER

P.O. Box 617
Hogg Building
Jackson, Kentucky 41339

ATTORNEYS
Robert H. Cornett (606)666-4821
Stanley T. Turner (606)666-4321

OF COUNSEL
James S. Hogg (Ret.)

Dear Mr. Carpenter,

I would very much like to order another copy of Kentucky Courthouses. Please send me an order form.

Thanks

Stanley T. Turner

P.S. Its a marvelous book!